The
LEAST
of the
LEAST

From Crime to Christ

WYATT ALLEN

Remnant
Publications

ACKNOWLEDGMENTS

Neither this book, nor the story it contains, would be possible without the help of some wonderful people that crossed my path at providential times. I wish to thank them for who they are and what they've done to bless my life. Therefore, I humbly acknowledge:

Jesus, for Your grace and mercy;

Mom, for your prayers and patience;

Tavia Wilson, for your compassion and care;

David Misenko, for your ministry and brotherhood;

Doug Graybill, for your friendship and wisdom;

Tommy G., for your advice and mentorship;

Neil Dye, for your trust and guidance;

Deb Davis, for your encouragement and support;

Walt Erickson, for your kindness and teaching;

Chris Chung, for your seeking me out and publishing this book;

Debi Tesser, for your suggestions and ideas;

And to my wonderful wife, Jenni Allen, for your constant love and companionship.

And for the countless others that have shown me true Christian love, thank you!

CONTENTS

1 On the Run 7

2 At the Nightclub 9

3 Growing Up. 13

4 Into Trouble. 21

5 Rehab 25

6 Detention. 31

7 A New Journey.. 35

8 The Journey Continues 41

9 Learning the Way. 45

10 Figuring It Out 49

11 Radio Preaching 51

12 Meanwhile 57

13 Death and Hell.. 61

14 God Wanted My Time 69

15 I Believe.. 77

16 Providence at Work 79

17 Now an Adult 83

18 Jail-House Religion. 91

19 Being Judged 97

20 The Big House 101

21 The Last Stop.. 107

22 Learning and Growing. 113

23 Tested and Tried 119

24 Reflecting... 125

25 An Inside Job... 129

26 The Board... 133

27 And a Wake Up.. 137

28 I'm Out!... 141

29 A Budding Relationship................................ 145

30 Our Courtship 151

31 An Engaging Woman 159

32 God Meant It for Good 167

33 The Least of the Least 171

34 Principalities and Powers 175

35 Be Thou My Vision 179

36 Going Forward.. 181

Appendices 183

Chapter 1
ON THE RUN

Running from the cops at full speed, I ducked into a nightclub for teenagers called Silverado's. Out of breath and still "high" on drugs, I went to the bathroom to wash my face. The noise of heavy metal shook the air. Taking it all in, I could hear my heartbeat throbbing in my head. It was a close escape.

I was fourteen years old and deep into the party scene. Just six months earlier, I had begun smoking weed. I loved the feeling it gave me. In my chaotic life I needed this relaxing drug. What started out as a weekend of pleasure quickly turned into a daily obsession. It was with an almost animal passion that I craved my next "high." If I had to steal, lie, or hurt someone, it didn't matter; I was going to have my drugs. As my life showed, it often came to this.

I styled myself a "head-banger." Imagine me flailing around as heavy metal filled my soul. I danced violently as I was flooded with passion for my favorite music. We were few in number, those of us who shared the taste for music that would give anyone else a headache, but we loved it. I was making new friends, and I felt welcomed. I was home.

Some of these new friends were involved in Wicca or witchcraft, otherwise called the occult. The occult. The name itself was fascinating to me. I would spend hours and hours reading books on the matter. My brother had a book called *Modern Magick*, and after he had read and discarded it, the book fell into my hands. I was mesmerized as I read about the Kabbalah, how to read Tarot cards, how to evoke spirits to do my bidding, and other rituals that would grant me the power I had only encountered in my dreams.

As I shared my budding beliefs, I enjoyed seeing the shocked reactions from professed Christians and other self-assured individuals. My own family, especially my mother, was greatly concerned by my changing disposition. I didn't see myself as evil as others saw me. Practitioners of witchcraft, usually called Wiccans or pagans and sometimes druids, still maintain a code of ethics. This code boils down

7

to virtually one rule, called the Wiccan Rede: "An' harm ye none, do what ye will," which means that if it doesn't harm anyone, do as you please—no restrictions to burden you, no laws to obey, within reason. I thought freedom was gained by having no restrictions and no responsibilities. I was soon to realize how wrong I really was.

Not all head-bangers are considered Goths, and not all Goths are into the occult, but many are. I was one who began to embrace it all.

This dark trend consists mostly of a black gloomy style of dress. For Goths, just about everything is black, especially the fingernails and the clothes. On party nights, my friends and I would go even further and paint our faces and lips black. To emulate Brandon Lee from the movie *The Crow*, with his whitish face and black tear streaks, was considered extreme. But sometimes we would even go that far. If this wasn't enough, we would give each other sinister tattoos and body piercings. The changes were gradual, and I noticed that the more edgy I became, the more attention I received. I didn't realize at the time just how much attention I really craved.

I was seeking belonging; I desired acceptance. I never would have admitted it at the time, but this ninth-grader was lost and was grasping for anything he could reach. Marijuana, witchcraft, music, and friends failed to truly satisfy, so I stayed on the run. I was running from a past I didn't understand and toward a future that was just as confusing. Nevertheless, I kept running.

Chapter 2
AT THE NIGHTCLUB

At the nightclub after dodging the police, I emerged from the bathroom in a cold sweat. All the Goth makeup was now removed, and I began to look for a place to lay low for a while. Across the room, there were a couple of tables, but neither of them was empty. At one sat a lone man dressed in a long black trench coat. Though he had a sharp goatee and a bald head, he seemed approachable enough. Looking up from reading a book as I approached, he didn't seem to mind my indicated desire to sit down. My brain dull and sluggish from smoking weed all night, still in an adrenalin-induced daze, I tried to recap the last twenty minutes in my mind.

It was after 11:00 P.M. Several of my friends and I had been out having fun, riding around town and generally getting high and goofing off. We had decided to go to Silverado's, just hang out there, and then go where the night took us. We drove into a parking garage and parked near the stairs. We were about to take our last hits of the joint when we saw the unmistakable lights of a patrol car fill the underground garage. If we weren't already scrambling by then, when he sounded his siren, all was chaos. We opened our doors in a flash, and it was every man for himself.

The only way out was up the flight of stairs and onto the side street. I was running and digging through my pockets at the same time to ditch my drugs and paraphernalia. I lost sight of everyone else, but I didn't dare look back, imagining that any second a strong hand would come down hard on my shoulder, bringing me to a sudden stop. Rounding the corner of the building, I was glad to see only a few people in line waiting to get into the club. With my hand stamped, and my heart beating out of my chest, I made my way downstairs to the bathroom, hoping I had not been seen. I figured I stood out a little bit from the others around me because of the black paint on my face. The next thing I knew, I was sitting down with this dark, somber-looking man. My heart was still racing when he engaged me in conversation.

He spoke first: "You seem troubled. Tell me what's on your mind."
I was still noticeably shaken.

"The cops are after me," I said in a hushed tone, wondering if I would regret telling him.

"I see," he said.

We sat in silence for a minute or so before he spoke up again: "Here, I have something for you."

He took some kind of dry herb out of his pocket, sprinkled it into his almost-full cup of coffee, and slid it over to me.

"What is it?" I wanted to know.

"Something that will help you to calm down."

Doubtful, but appreciating his confident helpfulness, I took it, and we continued to sit in silence as I sipped the concoction. I was still worried that the police might find me. A few minutes later, he broke the silence by asking me with a sly smile, "Friend, do you know much about Satanism?"

I had never given much thought to Satanism except in passing. I knew people had confused my occult practices with being satanic, but I didn't even believe in a devil. The extent of my experience with Satanism reached as far as my music, as several of my favorite bands were professed servants of Satan. But I was certainly no "Satan worshiper." Though I didn't know much about it, I instinctively knew it was forbidden, even dangerous. I had read about the powers of black magic, but was never brave enough to venture into investigating them. Even our books on magic and witchcraft would warn us away from such dark arts. But this night, I figured I had nothing more to lose, so I told him, "I've heard about it. What do you know?"

Erik, as he called himself, spoke for a while about the philosophies and concepts behind *The Satanic Bible* and Satanism. Much of it was over my head and hard to take in, but I understood enough of what he was saying to see that the power available in following Satan was greater than that which could be found by praying to the varied gods of witchcraft. In fact, in my short time of dabbling in paganism, nothing clearly supernatural had happened, nothing that couldn't be explained away as coincidence or happenstance.

Even as I was considering these things, Erik invited me to participate in a ritual with him that he promised would take away my nervousness. He could see that I was still a little skittish from the run-in with the law. He intrigued me by his methodical, almost mesmerizing speech. After thinking about it for a second and reasoning that it couldn't hurt, I agreed. So we began.

He retrieved a small noose and dagger from inside his trench coat and explained that he needed a symbol of death to make the ritual work. He then laid it on the table and instructed me to position my hands, like his, over the noose, making the sign for the element water, and to repeat after him. The spell began by invoking Satan, using several of his names. As I echoed him in both Latin and English, I realized I was praying to the devil!

The ceremony was very solemn, and though there were people around, it seemed we were in our own little world. Pushing aside questioning thoughts, I finished the ritual with him. To my amazement, all of a sudden I felt calm and sober. "Surely there is power in such rituals," I thought. "Satan can't be all bad if he can cause the peace I felt."

Erik and I talked for a little longer after the spell had worked its charm. That night I resolved to pursue Satanism and see how I could tap into the power that this new path promised.

As soon as I could, I purchased my very own copy of *The Satanic Bible* by Anton Szandor LaVey, who was called the black pope. I read it with great interest. I had to hide the book from my mother, as I did all my other demonic possessions such as my death-metal music CDs and morbidly-themed clothes. I never officially joined the Church of Satan. To join you must pay $200 and be older than 18. I lacked the money and the age to qualify, but that didn't stop me from professing my new-found religion at school and among my friends. In fact, I met a couple of people about my age who were already practicing. I was happy to learn.

We spent the evening at Chris's house goofing off, getting high, and snorting some lines. As it got late, we mellowed out and Chris asked me how serious I was about being a Satanist. I insisted I was very serious and was learning more all the time. "Okay then. It is time we receive a sign to prove it!" He was talking about the symbol of Satanism, the upside down pentagram. We chose a place on our legs and agreed to give each other a tattoo of the mark of our new master.

I had never received a tattoo before, but I didn't think they were supposed to hurt so much. Of course, using a sewing needle and homemade Indian ink didn't help. But I felt proud to bear this token of my devotion. Surely the prince of darkness would take me seriously now.

Though all those around me, my family, my old friends, my classmates, and teachers, seemed concerned with my new fascination,

I affirmed that I was having the best time of my life. Every counsel they gave and warning they sounded came across like Charlie Brown's teacher. I was being strengthened by Satan to do evil, inspired to commit crimes for which I was never caught, and motivated to hate without remorse. The deeper I delved into Satanism, the more rebellious I became. Being full of this rebellious spirit, it was not long before I started to reap unexpected consequences.

Chapter 3
GROWING UP

A ngela Rose, my mother, was born into a devoutly Roman Catholic family. Her father, Donald LaRoque, was born and raised on the Fort Peck Reservation. He died when she was just six years old, leaving my grandma to raise my mom and her sister alone in Milwaukee, Wisconsin. Mom attended a private Lutheran school because she was expelled from public school in fifth grade for setting a garbage can on fire. Meanwhile, for her mom, drugs became a source of income as well as a temporary relief from the pressures of life and from my mother's incessant epileptic spells. It wasn't hard for her to sell drugs in the late 1960s, and business was booming. When she received news of an imminent bust, Grandma found it necessary to get out of town. She took her girls and moved to a little town near Rolla, Missouri in about 1977.

Not long after they had arrived and Mom had gotten settled into school, her schoolmates eagerly introduced her to Albert Allen. She was fourteen and he was twenty-two years old. He was just finishing his four-year enlistment and was being honorably discharged as a corporal in the United States Marine Corps. Returning troops were town heroes and my dad-to-be was no exception.

He had grown up in a large family as the eldest of five. As soon as he could, he'd signed up for the Marines. At this time, the Vietnam War was just winding down. Nevertheless, the violence he witnessed and experienced during this time no doubt played a major role in his future as a husband and father. Besides the violence, he also brought home from the war a heavy taste for drugs. But drugs cost money, so to support his habit he began to sell them. My grandmother, needing drugs to use and sell, would buy them from Albert. This worked out splendidly for both of them.

When he saw that my mom was not being treated well or even being fed at times by her mother, he expressed his concern. Still, the neglect continued. At this time, it seemed that the only person who cared for my mother was Albert. Sure, he had a taste for alcohol and drugs, but so did every other person in Mom's life. In caring for her, he always made sure she got to school and had food. For my mother, it was the best of a bad situation. Her neglect, hunger, and a desire for nurture left her lonely and vulnerable. Then along came Albert, who truly seemed to care. So a relationship began. Grandma couldn't be happier to be rid of Mom and freely emancipated her. So in July of 1978, when Mom was fifteen, they were married in a small Baptist church in Jerome, Missouri.

Two years later, Mom had her first child, Dustin. She couldn't have been happier with the red-haired baby. Her family was now growing. He had just turned two when I, Wyatt Edward Allen, was delivered to Mrs. Angela Rose Allen and Mr. Albert Edward Allen on December 10, 1982. Jasmine Kay, my blond-haired sister, followed about three years later. Together we faced a world of pain and suffering mixed with hard work and sacrifice. We did the best we could with what we had. However, there was trouble from the start.

I loved my father. From my angle, he was my caretaker and provider. My memories of him are mostly good, although in those days I did my best to block out and forget about the bad. I had to do a lot of blocking out and forgetting.

There was not a time when my parents were together that there was not trouble at home. Dad had an extremely bad temper, and combined with his drug and alcohol use, he became even more dangerous. Our whole family suffered from his violent outbursts and drunken rages. Even with his unfaithfulness to my mother and his continued abusive behavior toward her and us, she was determined to hold the family together for the sake of us children.

At one point, Dad, his brother and some of his friends robbed a house and burned it down to cover their tracks. Although they were all caught, most of the others received the blame for the crime, with my uncle having to do hard time in prison, while Dad only had to do several months of jail time despite being the probable ringleader.

My mom was hoping and praying that his time away from her and us kids would give him the opportunity to wise up and get his life together. When she found out that while in jail he had received a visit from a Baptist preacher and was reading his Bible, she was overjoyed. During her visits with my dad, he would give every assurance that he would be a changed man and would stop drinking. She clung to this hope for months, finally imagining a normal life for her family.

The day Dad was released after spending about six months in jail, he returned to the liquor store and bought a fifth of whisky. He came home drunk and went right back to how he was before. Mom couldn't stop the beatings she would receive at his hands, though she prayed and pleaded for mercy. The alcohol blinded him to reason and judgment. It always did. Jasmine was but a year old at this time.

Dustin was so happy to see Dad. Now Dad could help him fix his bike. But the day after Dad arrived home, he didn't have time to fix the bike. He didn't have time the next day either. But on the third day, Dad was under the car trying to fix some problem when Dustin again thought to ask Dad about his bike. Already frustrated, Dad lost control and began shouting at Dustin. Working himself into a frenzy, Dad went over to the bike, picked it up, and from across the driveway threw it right into Dustin, knocking him breathless onto the gravel. As Dustin lay on the ground crying and bleeding, Dad went back to working on the car.

At that point, Mom had had enough. For the safety of us children and herself, she planned an escape. Previous attempts had landed her in the hospital, or worse yet, waking up hours later in a pool of dried blood—her own. Dad would even go to bed with his hand bound tightly around her wrist, knowing she wanted out.

The plan went into effect about 4:00 in the morning on an early summer day in 1987—the same day the welfare check was to come in. Dad had come home drunk after midnight and quickly passed out. Mom had secretly been packing stuff away since she determined to leave him, hiding it here and there.

Having no vehicle, she was compelled to take Kenny's car. Kenny lived just next door and was renting his trailer to us. He had let her use the car in the past, and it seemed to be the only option. Thankfully, he had left the keys in the car. Knowing he was a good man, Mom quietly packed the station wagon, woke up Dustin and me, and carried Jasmine to the car. Then we were off.

We hid behind the post office until it opened at 6:00 AM. Mom feared that Dad would find her, and she trembled to think of what he would do to her when he did.

She needed that check to buy food for us and diapers for Jasmine. The postwoman finally arrived. Mom explained the situation to her, and with sympathy the woman did her best to find the check. In the meantime, she treated us kids to some cookies. With the check in hand, Mom stopped by the county sheriff's department to let the officers know what we were doing because the store did not open until 8:00 AM. The trouble was that law enforcement could not do anything until something happened, so she cashed the check and went to the store. We arrived at Food for Less, the small town grocery, and waited anxiously for it to open at 8:00. Dustin and I were told to stay in the car and keep the doors locked. She took Jasmine, just a little more than a year old, with her into the store. We're not sure how he found us, but while she was in the store, Dad began knocking on the car window for us to let him in. We didn't know what to do—obey mom or obey dad? We were too afraid to do anything. At only four years old, I held tight to my brother in the middle of the car. Finally giving up on us, Dad waited for mom to come out of the store. She had no idea he was there.

As she walked out of the store, he caught her and smacked her hard across the face. Shoving her to the ground and yelling at her, he started to kick her. Jasmine, sitting in the cart, was bawling.

Many people watched this whole scene, and finally a man said that he had called the police. Dad just yelled after that, insisting that she give him whatever money she had left and demanding that she return home. At last, the police arrived and Mom was able to load the car and leave, flabbergasted that he wasn't even arrested!

She left the parking lot, but where should she go? She had to call our landlord, Kenny, to let him know that she had taken his car. They agreed to meet at a local pizza place where we were to wait. When Kenny arrived, he bought us all pizza and offered to let us stay at Lake of the Ozarks in his parents' trailer on a temporary basis. We spent a few months there until my parents' divorce was finalized at the end of that August. Mom was resting easy far away from Dad.

We eventually returned to Rolla, hoping things would settle down. Mom applied for assistance and received help in getting a small house. Dad wanted to reconcile. To try and convince her he was changing, Dad began attending an alcohol treatment program while we were away and begged Mom to go to family counseling with him. She refused. He'd had his chance, she said. Dad made many promises, but when those proved ineffective, he used threats. He finally realized he needed serious help, so he checked himself into a psychiatric hospital. He was diagnosed with bipolar/manic depressive disorder and given lithium.

One night, Dad disappeared from the hospital. Out of concern for my mom, the doctor called her to warn of his disappearance. Sure enough, that next morning dad kicked in our house door and held us hostage. He pulled the phone from the wall and forbid anyone from going in or out. After four days, he left in a rage.

Dad, seeing alcohol as the poison that was destroying him, joined Alcoholics Anonymous (AA), hoping to quit. His joining AA resulted in a bit of a reprieve.

Nevertheless, the harassment didn't end. Mom found an opportunity and moved us to Jefferson City, Missouri, about an hour and a half north. She worked hard to provide for us, first as a waitress, then as a factory worker. We lived in the projects on Chestnut Street.

Because Mom was at work a lot and our babysitters were more interested in their boyfriends than us youngsters, Dustin and I would often run around town. Our fingers were sticky when we went into stores. We would steal toys and food from the local Gerbe's department store, filling our coats time after time. One time we even got caught but were able to get away by giving false information. We rode our bikes everywhere and played around museums, parks, water drains, and friends' houses. I even remember throwing rocks over the prison walls, not knowing what was on the other side. We played all around the capital building, walking anywhere we wanted to go. Hotels were especially fun. I'm convinced that soda machines invented the anti-theft mechanism because of us. We would stick our skinny little arms up inside the machine and pick any soda we wanted.

Such freedom eventually led to trouble at an old house we thought was abandoned. Playing with fire and with some old furniture on the back porch, we would burn this or that, which never amounted to much until one day after some of the neighbor kids had been playing there with us. We were tired of amusing ourselves with oil and a certain couch, so we left. Suddenly we heard the sound of sirens and saw smoke. No! It couldn't have been where we were playing! But sure enough it was! We immediately fled the scene.

Later that day, there was a knock at the door. There stood a couple officers with their shiny badges and serious looks. Apparently, a little girl had blamed the whole thing on my brother and me. My first ride in a police car quickly followed. The fire consumed the entire house, which was occupied, but thankfully no one was home. We were eventually taken home, but my mom felt a strong sting when a judge decided to make us kids wards of the court.

Mom began to work even harder. She worked doubles almost every day and even triples when she could get them. Because of this, she was able to get a house over on the west side of town in the suburbs. Her life was coming together. Dad's life seemed to be getting more stable too. A custody arrangement was worked out, and Dad started taking us every other weekend.

While Dad had us, Mom would work as many hours as she could. One Sunday, when Mom had just gotten off of a triple shift, she dropped into bed dead tired. She knew, though, that Dad would arrive at 9:00 to drop us off, so she set her alarm. The trouble was that Dad showed up at 8:00.

Dad knocked on the door and rang the doorbell. No answer. He knocked louder. Still no answer. He yelled and was getting more agitated by the second because he knew she was in there. Dad's solution was to break in through the garage door, kick in the downstairs entrance, and search for Mom. She had no idea anything was wrong until she was brutally awakened by Dad grabbing her and dragging her into the kitchen.

At one point, he picked her up and threw her to the ground. Her scream pierced the air as her tailbone shattered. Crying in pain, she reached for the phone to call the police, but he snatched the phone from her hands and began beating her in the face with it. All of us kids were crying hysterically, begging Dad to stop!

When he finally felt he had done enough damage, he left. The police came and went, and Mom went to the hospital where she spent the next month, while we stayed in a foster home. Mom lost her job, and to add to her misery, someone flooded our house while she was in the hospital.

These were our rough beginnings, yet as dysfunctional as we might have been, we always had food on the table and clothes on our backs.

It might seem from the stories of my past that my dad was a monster. Still, I loved my dad, and as confused as I was about how to relate to him, I believe he loved me the best he knew how. His own upbringing had, after all, been filled with episodes of trauma and drama.

It is amazing how quickly children forgive. Despite all the abuse, I loved spending time with Dad. We would fish together, hunt together, and even work together as he taught me how to be a carpenter like he was.

Dad eventually started to get clean. He received his one-month clean token from AA. Then he celebrated being six months clean. Before long, he was sober for two years and more. He was a totally different guy when sober, even though he still had a terrible anger problem. There were many times that we just spent father-and-son time together, time that did more to shape me than he or anyone realized. From the age of seven until I was fifteen years old, I moved between my dad's place around Rolla, Missouri, and my mother's place about six times. During this time, I continued to act out. I smoked my first cigarette at age seven. I was a terror to my teachers starting at age nine. At age twelve, I was arrested for burglarizing a house on Christmas Eve. Soon afterward, I was diagnosed as having ADHD (Attention Deficit Hyperactivity Disorder). I was constantly causing trouble at school, my grades were terrible, and I loved to fight.

Toward the end of the eighth grade when I was fourteen, I found my dad's stash of marijuana, so I stole some and tried it for the first time. I was immediately hooked—I loved it! He had so much that I was able to steal pounds of the stuff and smoke it, sell it, and give it away. For the first time in my life, I felt like I was accepted; I enjoyed the attention I received. I had always felt like an outcast, but finally I had people who actually liked to be around me (or at least my drugs—but that didn't matter to me).

Chapter 4
INTO TROUBLE

In October 1997, weeks after my narrow escape, I was arrested with so much marijuana in my possession that if I had been an adult, I would have received a large prison sentence. However, after spending just a few hours in the juvenile detention center, I was released with only a warning. Of course, I attributed this to my newly found religion. I did not realize that the Scriptures had said thousands of years before: "Because the sentence against an evil work is not executed speedily, therefore the heart of the sons of men is fully set in them to do evil" (Ecclesiastes 8:11).

This was just the beginning of my downward spiral. Mom was completely unaware, or so I thought, that I was sneaking out of the house most nights to party and have "fun." Early one morning before the sun came up, however, I returned to find that my room light was on. I feared the consequences and decided to avoid any punishment by just going back to the party and staying at my friends' houses for a while.

I didn't realize what this would do to my mother. She called every person I had ever known and put up "missing" signs with my picture on them. She spent several nights in tears and prayers, waiting and hoping for her son to return home. Nevertheless, even after I heard about the signs on store windows, I refused to go home. My heart of rebellion was set. Where my mom wanted me was at home where there were no drugs or parties.

While on the run, sometimes narrowly escaping the cops, I would camp under basement pool tables, in the RV that was parked in front of my friend Scott's house, or even in tents out in the woods. One time five of us slept the night in the front cab of an S10 pickup. Not my best night of sleep, I must say.

My escapade ended late one night at Earthquake Hollow in New Bloomfield, Missouri. Several of us, high on weed, decided to camp deep in the woods in this conservation area. We hiked twenty minutes or so down a steep valley and up the next ridge. We started a fire, and all was going well until the sun started going down. Everyone left because of the cold except Scott and me. The day had started out nicely, getting up into the 60s. We were determined to stay the night, but we had underestimated two things: how cold it would get and the availability of fire wood. It was pitch black because of an overcast sky, we didn't have a flashlight, and our little lighter wasn't going to do much to light the way home, but we knew we had to leave.

I got the idea to take my shirt off, wrap it tightly around a stick, and use it as a torch. We knew it would only burn so long, so we planned to run as fast as we could by the light of the burning cotton shirt. Sure enough, the shirt began falling to pieces as we made our way down one steep hill and up the other. We eventually had to grope the rest of the way. When we arrived, I was surprised to find the police just pulling in.

The officer called me over and asked, "Who are you, young man?" I was compelled to give him the answers he wanted, but I really wanted to know how he'd found me. He handcuffed me on the spot and put me in the patrol car. Ten minutes later, driving at 90 miles an hour, we arrived at the police station.

The senior officer on shift called my mom, and after talking to her, attempted to stage a one-on-one intervention. He showed me the most graphic pictures of a man who had committed suicide. Then he showed me the autopsy photos. While we waited for mom to show up, the officer was doing his best to lecture me as to the right path in life, warning me that if I didn't change, I could end up like this man—dead. As grossed out as I was by the pictures, it didn't change anything in me. Neither did his lecture have an effect. I didn't want to change!

Mom came. She immediately took me to Charter Psychiatric Hospital and committed me. She was at her wits' end! Before this, I had been in and out of psych wards, psychiatrist offices, and even committed for two weeks at a different mental hospital. I had already been diagnosed with ADHD when I was 12, but the mental hospital confirmed it again. They then added several other diagnoses, and after I left I was taking Adderall, Risperdal, and Prozac. Imagine taking these strong psychotropic drugs along with mind-altering marijuana and harder drugs! There wasn't much that Charter could do to help more than was already being done.

They didn't hold me long, and with my promises and professed desire to change, they let me go back to live with my mom. However, that very night, I packed my backpack and took off. I wasn't planning on going back, but after five days I was located again and detained in the juvenile hall. I failed a drug test but was again released. This happened four times before they decided I needed help. I was sentenced to complete drug rehabilitation in Springfield, Missouri. I had never sunk as low as I did there.

Chapter 5
REHAB

Rehab was very difficult for me. The program was called CSTAR (Comprehensive Substance Treatment and Rehabilitation), a two-month program. With my rebellious nature, it was hard for me to restrain from mischief. However, looming over my head was a warning from my juvenile officer in Jefferson City. If I failed the program, all my troubles from the past would catch up with me, and I would be put away for a long time. I didn't take that threat lightly and tried really, really hard. Yet try as I might, that old sinful nature would rear its ugly head and win every time. The only power I had was to *do* evil, not to *overcome* it.

I was very bitter. First, they took my *Satanic Bible*. Then I was made to do chores, go to bed at an early hour, work hard, and worst of all not do any drugs. Daily drills would have us jogging two miles. Disobedience meant termination. I was miserable!

"The Walls"

About two weeks after I started the treatment program a tour was scheduled to visit the Missouri State Penitentiary, also know as "The Walls." I heard it was called "America's bloodiest 47 acres" because of the many murders and rampant violence it boasted. The rehab staff did its part to raise the hype about the place before we went. They even invited Lieutenant Mitchell—a large black man who wore a sharp white shirt and made it clear that he was to be taken seriously— to speak about what goes on there. He told us graphic stories of assault, rape and murder, and to make his point, he lifted his shirt to show a thick, four-inch scar, proof of being stabbed by an inmate. Then he opened a display and showed us dozens of makeshift weapons used to assault and kill other inmates and guards. He appealed to us to take our upcoming trip and becoming inmates ourselves seriously.

Our van with about fourteen of us kids arrived at around 5:00 in the evening. This was the same place where I used to throw rocks over the walls as a kindergartener. After all those years, I was going to be behind those same walls, even if it was just to visit. The object of this "scared straight" tour seemed to be to make us fear the place so much that we would reform our ways. I was so full of anger and rage that I wasn't scared, at least not that I would admit. If anything, I was a little fascinated by the place.

We were ushered down several long, blind hallways. We passed numerous inmates dressed in gray as we went. They weren't locked down in cells; they were wandering around free! It turned out that even some of those leading our group were also prisoners! The tour started by taking us to a large conference room where a couple of the inmates told us their stories.

One man had murdered a cop on the side of the road. Another young man who styled himself J-Rock and was seventeen years old (just two years older than I) had hit a man in a street fight, sending the man falling backwards and fatally hitting his head on the curb. They shared their stories and tried to convince us that we needed to change our lives or we would end up in similar consequences. Me—in prison? Serving hard time? It seemed far-fetched, but I continued to listen in silence.

After the lectures concluded, our inmate tour guides began to take us around the prison accompanied by Lieutenant Mitchell and our re-hab facilitators. Some of the cell-blocks were four stories high with hundreds of convicts in such a small area. The noise was deafening. As we walked just inches from the bars, the inmates would yell and scream at us. Our guides pointed out that this was a maximum security prison and that most of the inmates were never going to go home. They encouraged us not to get separated from the group. I was a little more unnerved than I had expected, though I tried not to show it.

During the visit to the prison, we were crammed into the old death-row waiting cells where those destined for the gas chamber would stay. They showed us the dining halls where so many fights and stabbings happened, and the prison yard that had one corrections officer for every seventy-five or so inmates. The smells were very unpleasant.

About half way through the tour, the guides stopped us and lined us up along a cold brick wall. Two very muscular black guys yelled out angrily, "We heard that there is a Satanist among you. Whoever you are, step forward!" Hesitatingly, I began to step forward, wondering who it was that they "heard" that from. I knew they were talking about me. Now, in front of the whole group, they started to publicly humiliate me.

"So you don't believe in God, huh?"

"How can you deny the existence of the One who made you?"

They harangued me with questions too fast to even try to answer. I thought, but didn't say, "First, if this is what Christians are like, so mean and cruel, I'm glad I'm not one. Second, if they think so much of God, why are they in prison? All Christians are hypocrites!" As *The Satanic Bible* says, "Before none of your printed idols do I bend in acquiescence, and he who saith 'thou shalt' to me is my mortal foe!"

To further humiliate me, they told me to take off my shirt, for it would fetch a price on the prison yard. Yelling, one of them told me to get down and do twenty push-ups. Seeing all the other kids looking at me, I couldn't help but turn as red as a beet. I was as angry as I have ever been. I wanted to rebel and tell them what I really thought, but I knew the rehab staff was watching and I knew the consequences for creating more trouble. I bit my lip and decided to play their game—this one, and all the rest—until I could get back to the real world. So I dropped and had completed about seven push-ups when the other inmate harshly told me to stand up. Relieved that it was over, I obeyed.

Then, the first guy, looking surprised, angrily asked me if he had given me permission to get up, and commanded me to get back down and complete my push-ups. This routine continued, making me look like a shirtless fool to all my peers. I was embarrassed beyond belief, and my rage boiled within me. Finally, a guard came over and "made" them stop. I realized later that this was a staged performance designed to teach me a lesson. The only lesson it taught me was that people are cruel in the name of God, and that they deserve my hatred, and, should the opportunity present itself, my wrath and revenge. Finally, Lieutenant Mitchell brought my shirt back and told me he'd had to buy it back from an inmate.

The cruelty wasn't finished yet. Another young man and I were singled out and taken aside from the group to a large prison house where other inmates tried to lecture us about stopping drugs and staying out of trouble. I was appalled when he took us down into the shower room where there were naked men everywhere. My heart was hardened even more. Their shock tactics had the opposite of the desired effect. Six hours after it began, the tour was finally over. We didn't get back to the rehab center until after 1:00 in the morning. There was no talking on the way back and I brooded the whole time with resentment and anger while trying to catch a little bit of sleep.

"The Grind"

We returned to the program, where I continued to endure the torture of being "fixed." The daily program started out with exercise in the parking lot. We would spend about an hour going through "the grind" as they called it: squats, lunges, jumping jacks, and laps around the parking lot. It wore us out, but complaining was not allowed.

Afterward, we would spend most of the day in classes on drug abuse and on how to live functional lives. I tried my best to not stir up trouble, but my nature was to be evil. I recall learning about a technique called delayed gratification. Practicing this would help me to remember that if I said "no" now, I could experience greater pleasure later. Marijuana, they said, might feel good at first, but in the long run it would cause all kinds of problems. If I gave up the temporary pleasure, I would have a much better life.

Somewhere deep down inside of me, the logic of what they were saying was appealing, but the problem was that I didn't care about the "good life" that they wanted me to have. I had no desire to live a life that was unselfish. I wanted to live my life my way, and I resented everyone who tried to force me to live it any other way. The satanic doctrine of thelema said that I was my own god and the world was to bow to my desires and my will!

With such an attitude, I was in a constant state of stress. I yearned for freedom from the oppressive environment I was constantly in. Even the kind deeds and genuine concern I received from some of the staff I took as mean and cruel. They didn't deserve my hate, yet it burned within my soul. Remembering the best I could from the satanic bible they took from me, I called down curses upon them and asked to be filled with demonic strength to sustain the torture I felt.

One staff member, Keith, was especially assigned to help me. He was known as a therapeutic parent. I made it clear that he was not my parent and I'm sure he could palpably feel that I despised him. Helping us kids was not all he did. He taught classes and played piano for his church, he taught karate, and he used sign language to interpret for deaf children. As nice as he was, every gesture of help was repulsed just as fast. I didn't want help!

One day I noticed a facilitator's pack of cigarettes out in the open. I was sure I could easily get away with taking some. Gathering the nerve, I did just that. A powerful rush came over me as I took the risk. I missed that exciting feeling I used to get when I would break into houses and steal people's belongings when they were not home. I enjoyed stealing the cigarettes even more than I did smoking them in the bathroom when I was supposed to be taking a shower.

More opportunities opened up to steal cigarettes over the next couple of weeks and I would smoke one almost every day. This was working out fine until one Sunday evening. The shower was running, and I was at the cracked window smoking when Keith knocked on the door and cracked it a little to ask me a question about some towels. Immediately, he could smell the smoke and, opening the door a little more, he saw me standing by the window. I was busted!

Keith looked really troubled, and after giving me a lengthy lecture, he told me to write an essay about why I shouldn't smoke and its dangers. He sat me down with a pen and paper and told me not to get up until it was complete. I begged him to not report it and promised I would never do it again. But he told me he had to, and despite my pleas walked away and made that phone call. At that point, Keith became the most hated person on earth.

I considered making a run for it and trying to get out of there. But I was in a big city far from home, without any money or food. I would surely be caught. Gritting my teeth, I wrote that essay in the most trite words I could come up with. But when that wasn't to his liking, Keith made me do it all over again. My blood was already boiling; now I was ready to get violent. This was a waste of my time.

Plans of hate and revenge came to mind, and a wicked plot began to develop. In my mind, I imagined myself killing Keith and then killing myself. He certainly deserved it, and whether I lived or died didn't matter. My life was over as it was. The more time that passed, the more satanic hatred began to well up within me. I couldn't see through the passion of my temper and rage. I prayed for satanic strength to carry out this plot against this man. Nothing could be heard, not even my own thoughts, as all was consumed in the mantra that kept pace with my quickening heart beat: "He must die! He must die!"

Sneaking into the kitchen, I smuggled a knife to my room. Then, when the time came, I invoked the power of Satan and Keith quickly fell victim to my attack. Oh, how I desired for this man to die! Though it happened like I was in a dream, it was more like a nightmare. The assault forever affected this man's life. With three deep wounds and several defensive cuts, he barely made it alive to the hospital. The same officer that saved Keith's life handcuffed me and took me to juvenile hall in Springfield, Missouri.

This was June 1, 1998—a day forever seared in my memory, a day never to be taken back.

Chapter 6

DETENTION

When I was arrested I was placed into a paddy wagon that reminded me of a dog-catcher's truck. It was all steel with a ledge seat that ran from front to back. There was nothing to hold onto, and no way to hold on even if there was. I managed to pull my handcuffs from behind me under my legs to the front. They didn't like that, and an officer got out and re-cuffed me—this time as tight as possible. As we drove away from the crime scene, the array of police lights that lit up the back of that paddy wagon like a disco hall began to fade. The drivers wasted no time getting to the detention center. As quick as it was, it would turn out to be the beginning of the longest ride of my life.

I was ushered from the wagon to a large holding cell. The police took the hand-cuffs off and left me in the charge of the juvenile custody staff. A man with red hair and a groomed beard introduced himself as Jeff. He told me to take all my clothes off and stand with my legs spread and my arms out. I felt as low as I ever had in my life. Defeated, I did as he asked. He sprayed me down with a foul smelling spray, explaining that it was all part of a routine check-in.

The detention cell where I was placed was small with a steel bunk, toilet, and sink—nothing else. For days, I sat in that cell alone, afraid, and hopeless. I continued to contemplate suicide. Besides, I reasoned, what use was I to this old world anymore? I wasn't sure if Keith had lived or died. I really didn't care at that point. I didn't care about anything. I was numb. If I felt anything, it was loneliness, and this was almost too hard to bear. Again and again suicide would come to mind, but there was no way to accomplish the act. I could not talk to anyone. I had no books, no newspaper, and no contact of any sort. It was maddening.

For sport and to pass the time, I took toilet paper, wet it, and wadded it up into little balls, which I began to shoot into the sink across the small room. Because I was monitored by a camera 24/7, a staff member saw me and confiscated the toilet paper. That forced me to request

31

toilet paper when I needed it, and I had to forfeit it when I was done. The only thing left to do was count the bricks on the walls.

Then, not realizing I would gain book privileges after so much time of being good, I carved into the paint on the steel bunk, with my fingernail, a picture of the satanic Sigil of Baphomet, which was the upside down pentagram image of a goat. This was the sign of the Church of Satan. When they moved me to a new cell, they discovered my defacement and lengthened my total lockdown status with no book privileges. The torture and loneliness continued. At least I had a new cell with a different number of bricks to count.

Hours ran into days; days into weeks. I couldn't tell you what day of the week it was if you had asked. I was miserably lonely. However, I had one thing to look forward to, one thing they didn't take from me—parents were allowed to call on certain days and at certain times. That time was coming up. I would get to talk to Mom. Why she even wanted anything to do with me, I'm not sure, but she did. She didn't scold me harshly, but rather, in her motherly way, she showed nothing but concern, love, and care. Just what I needed! I denied the whole crime and did my best to change the conversation. Unfortunately, the call was short—only ten minutes—and I would not be able to hear from her again for two more weeks.

I began to settle into a normal routine at the detention center. And as time passed, I gained some of the normal privileges, like a thirty-minute recreation period and lunches in a common hall during the weekdays. If we behaved and didn't cause trouble, we could watch a movie on the weekend. I even gained back my toilet paper privilege! Every other meal was in my cell. When I finally got book privileges, I devoured the books on the shelf. Sometimes I would read up to three of them a day, swapping them out as often as I could. I could lose myself in a fantasy or adventure book very easily. I didn't have to think about life or reality; I didn't have to consider my future or be reminded of where I was—at least while I was reading.

Even with the new distractions, I was still plagued with not knowing if my victim was alive or dead. What would my future be? Would I end up in prison? Would I ever be free again? Nobody had answers to any of my questions. A dark cloud was over me most of the time.

I was appointed a public defender who informed me that the prosecutor wanted to try me in an adult court. I was just fifteen, so my attorney thought it was unlikely that they would succeed, but we would have to wait for a certification hearing to determine this. If I was certified as an adult, I would go to an adult jail and face time just like anyone else who had committed the same crime. My lawyer didn't even care if I had actually committed the crime or not. This hearing wasn't about whether or not I was guilty, but about whether or not I was competent to stand trial as an adult.

Because of the immediate and severe consequences of acting out, I did my best to keep to myself and stay quiet. That wasn't too hard considering it was against the rules to talk to other juveniles about our personal lives or our crimes. I actually appreciated all my medications, which were dispensed like clockwork. They seemed to help keep me in a light daze that prevented me from thinking too seriously about what might lie ahead. But not enough.

I relived the scenes of that bloody night time and again. I would wake up in cold sweats, vividly seeing my crime replay before my face. Was it guilt or shame, or was I just sorry for getting caught? I wasn't sure, but I was starting to regret what I had done. I realized that whatever happened to me, the consequences would be heavy. I knew I deserved whatever I got. That is if they knew it was me. I had concocted a crazy story that I thought might exonerate me. My parents, loving, but wanting to believe the best about their boy, seemed to believe me. Even my newly-appointed lawyer believed my side, though it didn't matter to her because she was not trying to prove my innocence, just keep me from the adult court. Nonetheless, if anyone was naive, it was *me* in thinking I would get away with it.

While I thought I had everyone deceived, a heavy cloud of depression continued to settle over me. I knew all was not well for my future. I still desired suicide as a way out. Besides, I reasoned, it would force all those who had treated me so badly in life to feel sorry for me. It would even make them feel guilty for treating me like trash. On a personal level, I wondered if my life was even worth living. I considered that I would be doing the world a favor by quitting this life. In the midst of these mind ramblings, I thought, "At least I get to talk to Mom again tonight."

It was a normal conversation until she asked about what I had in my cell. I told her how small and plain it was, how my most comfortable furniture was my stainless steel commode, and exactly how many bricks were on the wall. She asked me, "Son, do they have Bibles there? Are you allowed to have them in your cell? It seems it would help pass your time until we go to court."

I had no need for such rubbish. She knew my involvement in Satanism and had tried many times to reach out to me. I resented her "pushing" me into religion, especially since it never did her any good, at least not that I saw. I had never seen it do anyone any good. Everyone I had ever met who said they were a Christian was a hypocrite. I had even smoked weed with church-goers. They would tell me that God said all the herbs were created to be good.

The fact remained that we were allowed to have Bibles, so I told her as much. "Yeah, we have them. Too many of them, in fact." I could look across the dayroom from the phone area to our only two book-shelves and see a whole row of Bibles on them. I knew they were there. It had annoyed me that they were taking the space of books I might be interested in reading.

"Wyatt, why don't you take one and try to read it?"

Was she crazy? Her question aggravated me, but how could I tell my mother no? So I lied.

"Okay Mom, I'll try," I said, without any real intention of actually doing so. "So when can you come for a visit?"

I tried to change the subject. She didn't press the issue, and we talked about the three-hour drive it would take her to come see me.

Chapter 7
A New Journey

As the days passed, I grew lonelier and lonelier. A couple of months had passed since I had committed my crime. In juvenile detention, juvie, it was the same routine day in and day out. Breakfast in the cell, hit the showers, lock-down, thirty minutes of recreation, lock-down, lunch in the dining hall, lock-down, school (sometimes), lock-down, supper in the cell, thirty minutes of recreation, lock-down. Every day was the same.

Strangely, every time I passed the bookshelf when I went to lockdown, I would get a sickening feeling in my stomach—the kind of feeling you get when you realize you forgot an appointment or locked your keys in the car. At least fifteen Bibles were there with different sizes and covers.

I admit I was curious, but mostly I was tired of all the nagging about it. *The Satanic Bible* says that the Christian Bible is a mass of contradictions. Supposedly, a lot of the mythology about the devil had its origins in the Bible. Then, there was some concern in that I had once heard a story about when a *Satanic Bible* was accidently set on top of a Holy Bible and had immediately caught on fire. Would it burn me if I touched it, as evil as I was? I seriously wondered.

For days, I wrestled with the idea of reading it. At last, as if on a covert mission, I worked up the nerve and snatched one of the Bibles from the shelf and rushed to my cell on my way to lock-down before anyone could see what I had done. I had decided, for purely intellectual reasons, to read the entirety to discover all the contradictions, errors, and mistakes. My plan was to prove that Book wrong at last. I planned to read it from cover to cover and be through with it forever. Once I had read it and was armed with this information, I would have ammunition to attack those well-meaning, but deceived, Christians and put their puny, weak religion to shame. So I began to read.

I read day and night, sometimes up to eighteen hours a day, only to be interrupted by my daily routine. After lights-out at about 9:00, I would stand for hours near my cell door to read by the light beaming in. I found that in reading so much I would often awaken in the morning, recalling my most recent dream, which consisted entirely of reading the Bible, as if I had taken a picture of it with my mind and could read it from there. I could even see in my mind the actual words on paper before the dream fully faded from my memory. I was dedicated to my purpose and intent as I scoured the Scriptures for any sign of error.

The version I grabbed by chance was the New International Version. It was a student Bible with side notes and moralistic stories scattered throughout to try to add to the Bible reading experience. The childish anecdotes and lessons weren't very helpful to me, though a helpful note would appear here and there that would give more background information, which made a story a little more understandable.

For the most part, I could neither prove nor disprove the fantastic stories it contained. I discovered that it was a lot like the fantasy books I had read, with strange stories of miracles and an overall storyline of loss and redemption. I started to wonder if all the fantasy books got their inspiration from the Christian Bible but twisted it enough to hide their origin.

This was a captivating journey that I was taking. At first I was fascinated by the incredible stories in Genesis. They were unbelievable, but somehow reasonable. God created the world in six days? A flood covered the entire world? All the world's languages originated at the tower of Babel by a miracle confusing the tongues? A woman turned to salt, fire from heaven, a man told to offer his son as a sacrifice? My jaw was constantly dropping. There was a strange thread that wove everything together, yet it was still too fantastic to believe.

As the stories continued, I felt some sympathy for Joseph in Egypt. Though he was innocent, he had experienced what I was now going through. I felt guilty when God gave the Ten Commandments. I laughed to read about a donkey rebuking a backsliding prophet. I was intrigued when the children of Israel went over the Jordan on dry land and then marched around Jericho to see the walls fall flat. Samson and Delilah reminded me of a cartoon I had seen as a kid.

This book wasn't at all what I was expecting. Once started, I wasn't even tempted to put it down. I was having too much fun. I wasn't accepting it as truth or as "God's Word," as I heard it called, but the more I read, the more that barrier was breaking down. I kept superimposing my life into the lives of the Bible characters. I would often see myself in them.

It was in reading First and Second Samuel that I became captivated with the story of David, the son of Jesse. His life had been one of faithfulness to his God. When he was just a boy, the prophet Samuel had anointed him as the future king. As a musician, he played to relax King Saul. David defeated Goliath, and would later fight in the king's army. Because of his many successes, he quickly rose to fame among the people. Saul, like a madman, became jealous and began to hunt David, murdering priests and any others who got in his way.

When Saul got word of where David was, David and his men would hide in the mountains and strongholds in the wilderness. But the day came when the king had to use the bathroom and happened to choose the cave that the son of Jesse was hiding in. This was the perfect opportunity for revenge. This was the day David could choose to stop running. I was rooting for David to kill his enemy, to give him what he deserved!

I thought of what I had read in *The Satanic Bible*: "Hate your enemies with a whole heart, and if a man smite you on one cheek, SMASH him on the other!; (sic) smite him hip and thigh, for self-preservation is the highest law!" (*The Satanic Bible*, 18). Who would pass up the chance to assassinate their assassin?

But that is exactly what David did! "The LORD forbid that I should do this thing to my master, the LORD's anointed, to stretch out my hand against him, seeing he is the anointed of the LORD" (1 Samuel 24:6). I couldn't believe it! He had him in his hand! Instead of destroying him, he gave him *mercy*. Mercy.

Then it hit me. I desired mercy. I didn't want to get what I deserved. I realized that I deserved to be punished with death, but I desired to live and not die. I didn't want to spend the rest of my life in a cell like I was in. I wanted to be free. Something was happening in me. A few chapters later, when I read of another occasion where David could have killed Saul, but again granted him mercy, I had a little more understanding.

David was different from most of the other Bible characters I had been reading about. I didn't understand everything I read, but I could see that when a person put God first, God blessed him. David seemed close to God, so close in fact that Scripture says he was "a man after His own heart" (1 Samuel 13:14).

When I arrived at 2 Samuel 11, I was stunned at what I read. David, a faithful servant of God, was playing Peeping Tom with his neighbor's wife. She was "very beautiful to behold," it says. After finding out whose wife she was, the king sent his people to get her. He slept with her and sent her home.

When King David got word that she was pregnant, he concocted a plan to make her husband think it was his kid. Uriah returned from battle at the king's command and, after some small talk, David sent him home with plenty of food. I guess he figured that Uriah thought like he did and would want to be with his wife on his furlough from war. But he found out the next morning that his faithful soldier didn't go home but instead stayed at the door of the king's house.

A second attempt involving getting Uriah drunk also failed. So to solve his problems, David devised a murder plot like something you would see on TV. He sent Uriah back to the front lines with a letter for Joab, the captain of the army, who would seal Uriah's doom—put him in the heat of battle and pull back just in time to put him in the most danger. His plan worked and Uriah was killed with an arrow (not to mention others killed in the collateral damage). Then he married Bathsheba, Uriah's wife. Wow!

Adultery and murder. God's man was guilty of both! At first I felt disgusted that one with such a high profession should be such a hypocrite. But then I saw that "the thing that David had done displeased the LORD" (2 Samuel 11:27). If God was upset with David, all I could think about was how God must be upset with me. If everything I was reading was true, then I must be the most wicked boy on earth. If I had felt low before, now I felt completely hopeless. But I read on.

God sent a prophet named Nathan to show David his sin and to point it out in a clever way. How could he not have seen it? How could I have not seen mine? The rebuke was to the point: "You are the man... Why have you despised the commandment of the LORD, to do evil in His sight?" (2 Samuel 12:7–9). God pronounced judgment on David and his house, and told him that "because by this deed you have given great occasion to the enemies of the LORD to blaspheme, the child also who is born to you shall surely die" (verse 14).

I could tangibly feel God saying to me, "You are the man!" I felt condemned. David must have felt the same way because he immediately confessed his sin. But he was not long without hope. Nathan, the prophet of God, declared to him, "The LORD also has put away your sin; you shall not die" (verse 13). Though he was still to suffer some consequences, he was forgiven.

So here was this high-professing saint of God who had fallen lower than low, committing the worst of sins, and could be forgiven? Could it be this simple? Could it be that maybe, just maybe, I too could be forgiven by confessing my sins? My heart was doing back flips in my chest as I was taking it all in. I felt so dirty, so evil. I wanted to be free from the overwhelming guilt I suffered from, yet I had so many doubts, so many fears.

I was directed by a little note in my study Bible to another passage in the Psalms that would forever change my life. These were the very words that David wrote in the aftermath of his crimes. Here is what I read:

Have mercy upon me, O God,

According to Your lovingkindness;

According to the multitude of Your tender mercies,

Blot out my transgressions.

Wash me thoroughly from my iniquity,

And cleanse me from my sin.

For I acknowledge my transgressions,

And my sin is always before me. …

Purge me with hyssop, and I shall be clean;

Wash me, and I shall be whiter than snow. …

Hide Your face from my sins,

And blot out all my iniquities.

Create in me a clean heart, O God,

And renew a steadfast spirit within me. …

Deliver me from the guilt of bloodshed, O God,

The God of my salvation,

And my tongue shall sing aloud of Your righteousness.

—Psalm 51:1–3, 7, 9–10, 14

Again I was pointed to more verses:

Blessed is he whose transgression is forgiven,
    Whose sin is covered.

Blessed is the man to whom the Lord does not impute
    iniquity,

And in whose spirit there is no deceit. …

I acknowledged my sin to You,

And my iniquity I have not hidden.

I said, "I will confess my transgressions to the Lord,"

And You forgave the iniquity of my sin. *Selah.*

—Psalm 32:1, 2, 5

I read these passages, not as merely words on paper, but as the cry of my own soul. In my mind, everything began to make sense. I could see it now; I could see that my version of God was wrong. I judged God based on His professed followers, and not based on the Book He gave us. I had made a decision before I had all the information. It was so clear now; I had been deceived. I had been fighting the truth and rebelling against reason. God wasn't out to make peoples' lives miserable. God wasn't chasing man to clobber him but to save him from his own destructive ways.

Step by step I was being called. Gradually my heart was melting by the light of God's Word. When I saw the light of God's character in its full strength, when I saw His love and compassion, His mercy and tenderheartedness, His grace and forgiveness, suddenly my war against the Creator ended and I surrendered to His side. I was heartbroken. In tears I fell to my knees and poured my soul out to God. I pled for forgiveness—the same as David had received. Surely, if he could be forgiven for his sins of adultery and murder, God could forgive a poor wretch like me. In the anguish of my soul, I confessed my crimes to Him who already knew all about them. I wanted to be cleansed; I wanted to be free!

In this moment I gave myself to Him wholly and unreservedly. I was His and He was mine. By faith, I embraced all that I had read to this point. I earnestly believed that God loved me as much as any who walked the earth and that His offer of pardon was as much for me as for anyone. I absolutely knew that with His help I could stop doing all the wickedness that I had done in the past. He could change me.

Oh, what a relief came to my sin-sick soul. In one moment, I was free from guilt and shame, from depression and hate. I had never, in my whole life, experienced such a wonderful change. Miracle of all miracles—instead of proving the Bible wrong, it proved me wrong! I was born again; I was free indeed!

Chapter 8
THE JOURNEY CONTINUES

The story of how I grew as a Christian is an interesting account of God's providence. I say Christian, but to be honest I didn't even know what one was. I knew that Jesus had something to do with it. I knew that He died on the cross, but why and how that played a part in my walk with God, I wasn't so sure. Who was this Jesus, besides a baby we see every Christmas lying in a manger? I couldn't wait to find out.

Besides not knowing too much about Jesus, I was virtually clueless about anything else that the Bible taught. What I knew of Christianity was based mostly on what I had seen on TV growing up. So in my mind, Christian equaled Catholic; I didn't know the difference. How that differed from a Baptist or a Methodist, I wasn't quite sure. Even though I associated Bible religion with Catholicism, I didn't know any more than exorcisms, water being poured over naked babies, and priests who wore white collars around their necks. Oh, and the Virgin Mary played a part in there somewhere.

From the first day I picked up the Bible until the day I finished it, I read with fervency. It took me a month to read the whole Bible, but such a quick read left me with more questions than answers. When I finally got to the New Testament, I was amazed to actually see who Jesus was. I had used His name as a curse word plenty of times, and I had known that He was an important Bible figure, but until I read the "Gospel According to Matthew," I did not learn just how wonderful He really was.

Wow! What a Man! What a God! To think, "God with us," was in a very literal sense. All of a sudden, I understood all the manger scenes: the shepherds came to worship the Baby because that Baby came from heaven to save all mankind from sin! The puzzle pieces were beginning to really fit together and I was seeing a picture of God and His great plan for my life. Then I was shocked to see the same story told again in Mark from a slightly different perspective. Then again in Luke! And then John! Point taken: Jesus' life very quickly became the point of the whole Bible.

I fell in love with this lowly Rabbi from Galilee. His teachings offered wisdom beyond anything I had ever read. His compassion for all with whom He came in contact spoke of a love that I had never seen before. Why had no one ever told me about Him? How was it that I had never heard the truths He taught? Why did men hate Him so? Why did *I* hate Him so? It was only because I did not *know Him*! "And this is eternal life, that they may know You, the only true God, and Jesus Christ whom You have sent" (John 17:3).

The book of Acts was where I saw some true Christians in action. They demonstrated the faith that I wanted to experience. The church in its infancy made the story of Scripture all the more real for me. God was using average folk, people with issues, problems, and not-so-pretty pasts. He even used a Christian killer named Saul. That gave me hope that He could maybe, possibly, use a sinner named Wyatt.

As I was finishing the rest of the New Testament, I got stuck a few times in Paul's writings. Sometimes he was crystal clear, but at other times my head was swimming with questions about what he was talking about. Yet those letters he wrote to the different churches left no doubt about his passion to see God's church prosper. He loved them. Saul's story reminded me of an account about Jesus and a woman who was a notorious sinner.

Simon was throwing a feast and Jesus was invited, but in came this sinner woman. She washed His feet with her tears, kissed them, and then anointed them with oil. While she was showing her devotion to her Master, Simon began to mumble about her reputation. Jesus, knowing his mutterings, told him a parable that would reveal to him his self-righteous, judgmental spirit. "'Therefore,' Jesus said, rebuking him, 'her sins, which are many, are forgiven, for she loved much. But to whom little is forgiven, the same loves little.' Then He said to her, 'Your sins are forgiven'" (Luke 7:47) (See Luke 7:36–50). Saul loved and served God much because he had been forgiven of much.

By reading further through Paul's epistles (letters), I learned the true meaning of love (1 Corinthians 13) and faith (Hebrews 11). He showed me that the church must be in unity and order. He also used so many terms that I had never even heard before: justification, sanctification, and predestination, among others.

At last, I reached the final book of the Christian Bible, of *my* Bible. Revelation, the book of prophecy, was so full of symbols and imagery that I wasn't sure what to believe: a wounded lamb, warring locusts, angels everywhere, a beautiful city from heaven, and a lake of fire. The chapters all sounded like the making of a Hollywood blockbuster.

What did it all mean? I wasn't sure, but I knew I wanted to find out. This incredible journey through the Scriptures left me aching for more. I knew I had much to learn. If I was to be a disciple of Jesus, I realized I needed to sit at His feet and be taught of Him. I committed to studying the Bible until I knew the truth of what it taught and I had discovered His plan for my life. Still, at this point I was loaded with many questions.

Chapter 9

LEARNING THE WAY

I had been in juvie for over four months now, and I now firmly decided that I wanted to be a Christian. I wanted to follow the teachings of Jesus and His disciples. I wanted to take up my cross and follow Him. Logic and common sense told me that there must be others out there who wanted to do the same. This book had so much power in it that I was sure anyone who read it would experience exactly what I did. In the loneliness of my cell, I yearned for that fellowship that the early church had experienced. I wanted to find others who were Christ's followers. But where were they?

I admit that I didn't have a lot of church experience, but I had seen a lot of Bibles. So I was at a loss to understand how it was that I had never met a Christian. Sure, I'd met many people who said they were Christians, but I couldn't ever recall meeting someone like Paul or Peter. I had never seen people behave like those in the Bible. Where were the zealous saints who wanted to tell the world about their resurrected King? I figured that in all the world there had to be many people who were following the Bible like in the book of Acts. They were called "the sect of the Nazarenes" (Acts 24:5), "the Way" (Acts 24:14), "the church of God" (Acts 20:28), and simply, "Christians" (Acts 11:26). So where did the names Baptist, Catholic, and Presbyterian come from?

Even though my whole family and many of my friends called themselves Christians, I did not see any resemblance in their lifestyles to that of Jesus, His disciples, or any of the saints of old. I couldn't recall which churches they went to (most never attended church). But where were the godliness and holiness I kept reading about? Where could I look to find them today?

I had honest questions that I was determined to find answers to. From what I knew of the movies, priests were not allowed to marry. But wasn't Peter married? Why did they talk about Mary the mother of Jesus so much and pray to her when the Scriptures said so little about her? Why were there always statues of Mary that people prayed to and worshiped? Weren't these statues called idols? Weren't they forbidden? Either I didn't understand something, or something was wrong—seriously wrong.

I know it sounds strange, but here I was, fighting against a church and a religion that didn't even reflect what the Bible really taught. Anton Szandor LaVey, author of *The Satanic Bible*, laid the foundation of his doubt by telling a story:

> On Saturday night…I would see men lusting after half-naked girls dancing at the carnival, and on Sunday morning when I was playing organ for tent-show evangelists (sic) at the other end of the carnival lot, I would see these same men sitting in the pews with their wives and children, asking God to forgive them and purge them of carnal desires. And the next Saturday night they'd be back at the carnival or some other place of indulgence. I knew then that the Christian church thrives on hypocrisy, and that man's carnal nature will out no matter how much it is purged or scourged by any white-light religion. (*The Satanic Bible*, 6–7)

And I thought that all Christians were like that. But this is not what the Bible teaches. From what I read in the Bible, people who behave like that will be cast into the lake of fire. God did not condone sin or rebellion. In fact, He gave Jesus to die because of the sins of man. For His followers to continue in the very same sins He died for is an affront to His love.

Would I have been so anti-Christian had I known what Jesus was really about, what He taught, and how much He loved? Would I have enjoyed my experiences at church much more if I had known that this was where God met with His people, and taught them in His way? My few memories of going to church as a kid consisted entirely of playing games, watching puppet shows, and doing crafts. I had no concept of God's high calling on my life. Praise God for the Bible!

I'm thankful that one of the first great truths I learned was that of the authority of God's inspired Word. The Bible could be trusted and relied upon (mankind not so much). I knew that whatever I believed, it should be based on its teachings. If God was going to be my Teacher, then the Scriptures would be my textbook. "Be diligent to present yourself approved to God, a worker who does not need to be ashamed, rightly dividing the word of truth" (2 Timothy 2:15).

It took a while before I told anyone of my conversion. Even though I wasn't ashamed, my pride held me back. I did not like to be wrong, and admitting that I was deceived was the hardest thing I could do. I was also worried. Would anyone believe that I was actually converted? Would my motives be doubted? I'd already heard the phrase "jailhouse religion" being floated around. I was known as a pathological liar, fully capable of making up a story to get my way.

One way or another, I was about to find out what others thought. Ringing in my ears was the verse, "If you confess with your mouth the Lord Jesus and believe in your heart that God has raised Him from the dead, you will be saved" (Romans 10:9).

I finally worked up the nerve, and the next time I spoke to my mother I told her about my conversion. In response, she went shopping. I was going to turn sixteen years old on December 10th and for a present she spent $70 and bought me a brand new, leather bound New King James Bible with cross references and study notes. When she was able to come and visit me from Jefferson City, she brought it with her. It took a little bit to get approval, but when I got it, I was so thankful! What a blessing! What a miracle! I could read the study notes at the bottom of the page and gain deeper insight into the meanings and backgrounds behind the text.

Not long afterward, she bought me a *Pictorial Bible Dictionary* and the *Strong's Exhaustive Concordance*. We were only allowed to have two books in our cell at any one time. Any extra property was to be kept in a small locker in the day room. Over the next several months, I very nearly wore out those books. I used the concordance to do subject studies on every topic I studied. Every answer I received opened more and more questions. I studied and studied. I came to realize that the church I thought was the Christian church couldn't even be using the same book. I wondered if it had a different Bible altogether. Come to think of it, I'd never seen any of my Catholic family even read from the Bible.

When I was no longer a closet Christian, I began to ask the other kids and some of the staff about religion. Thankfully, that was one of the things we were allowed to talk about, but I quickly found out that most didn't care about the Bible, and those who did, didn't care to talk about it. I did, however, discover a new word: denominations—and apparently there were a lot of them.

Just to prove it, a juvenile staff member brought in the faith direc-tory from the Life section of the *Springfield News Leader*. Turns out, Southern Baptists and Roman Catholics were not the only churches in town, though there were lots of those. There were also Methodists, Pentecostals, Mormons, Presbyterians, Anglicans, Adventists, and Assembly of God adherents. There were denominations called the Church of God, Church of Jesus Christ of Latter-day Saints, Church of Christ, Christian Church, and Christian Science. It appeared that not every believer agreed about what the Bible taught or even used the Bible.

Why so many churches? What were the differences? What did they believe? Which one was right? Did it matter? After contemplating these questions, I had a great idea: I would write all of these churches and ask them what they believed and taught. And that is just what I did.

Whoever had the truth, one thing was for certain, I needed to be baptized. John the Baptist baptized. Jesus' disciples baptized. Three thousand were baptized on the day of Pentecost after they believed the gospel. Paul and Peter said some powerful things about baptism. Even my new Lord and Savior was baptized! It was time to get wet. But how?

I knew it was appropriate to have someone else baptize me, but that was impossible in my situation. So I devised a plan that I hoped would work. After a season of prayer, committing myself to serve Jesus forever and repenting of all the sins I could recall, I arose from my bunk, went to the sink, and began to plug the drain holes with toilet paper. This was an especially solemn time for me. With holy anticipa-tion, I began to fill that shallow metal sink attached to the toilet with water. Finally, after a sufficient amount of water was in there, I dipped my hand into the water, raised it above my head, and slowly poured it over my hair while I said, in a whisper, "I baptize myself in the name of the Father," I reached for another handful, "and of the Son and," with a third scoop, I said "of the Holy Spirit."

I unplugged the drain and sat back down on my bunk with a sense of satisfaction. I'm sure now that the angels of God had a pretty good chuckle that day. I had a lot to learn.

Chapter 10
FIGURING IT OUT

About this time I was allowed to have a Walkman radio in my little cell, and my dad brought me one when he visited. This little device impacted my life in a definite way. On the low end of the FM dial were about five Christian stations; on the high end were music and sports stations of every kind. Very late at night, I was able to listen to preaching on the AM radio dial. I was skyrocketing upward in my Christian experience. I sat at the feet of Jesus every day by studying the Scriptures, and now I could hear solid Bible teaching where I could learn even more. However, the radio was turning out to be bittersweet.

For the first time in months, I was able to listen to the music I loved. Heavy metal and death metal were my style before my conversion. This was the first time my new faith collided with my previous lifestyle. I hadn't considered all the ways my life would change after becoming a Christian; I just knew that becoming a Jesus follower was the right thing to do. I knew that He alone could bring me lasting peace and eternal life.

At first I indulged; I bathed in the music I had been missing. Then the conviction came. The Spirit would not allow me to take pleasure in the things of the world. Echoing in my ears were the words of Scripture, "Do not love the world or the things in the world. If anyone loves the world, the love of the Father is not in him" (1 John 2:15). I clenched my teeth and made a resolution that I would, from that day forth, listen no more to worldly music. I was relieved and disappointed at the same time. But the peace finally came as I accepted that the Lord knows what is best for me.

That Saturday night, I was delighted to hear—for the first time ever—"Christian" heavy metal on one of the Christian stations. I was so thrilled! I could still have my favorite music but without the evil. For a couple of weeks, I treated myself to this special radio show each Saturday. I would head-bang and try to figure out the incomprehensible words and what praises they were singing (screaming), but something began to change. When I would hear the music, my whole disposition would change. I would feel sinister and wicked. Even when I could discern the spiritual words, I felt something was wrong. It was like the story of Nadab and Abihu when they offered profane fire on the holy altar of the Lord (see Leviticus 10).

I began to see that this was not the worship God wanted from me; He did not want His worship mingled with worldly methods, as he instructed the Hebrews when they were to take possession of Canaan land:

> Take heed to yourself that you are not ensnared to follow them, after they are destroyed from before you, and that you do not inquire after their gods, saying, 'How did these nations serve their gods? I also will do likewise.' You shall not worship the LORD your God in that way; for every abomination to the LORD which He hates they have done to their gods; for they burn even their sons and daughters in the fire to their gods. Whatever I command you, be careful to observe it; you shall not add to it nor take away from it. (Deuteronomy 12:30–32)

I learned that God's worship was just that—God's. It was not for me to decide what was appropriate and what was not. Me-centered worship was what got Lucifer into trouble. And when I was a Satanist it was what I desired. "God is Spirit, and those who worship Him must worship in spirit and truth" (John 4:24).

I went through the same experience with "Christian" rock and contemporary Christian music. I found out that just because something is called Christian doesn't necessarily make it so. I knew that being a Christian meant there would be sacrifices, but giving up my favorite (and even my not-so-favorite) music was a challenge. However, my commitment to follow the Savior was resolute. He helped me, and it wasn't long before the sad, old hymns of yesteryear became happy, beautiful songs, full of meaning and power. Like David with Saul, the heavenly music would drive temptation away. I even discovered some newer songs that had beauty and pathos that made me want to draw closer to Jesus and not the world. But it was the hymns that challenged me most.

> Let the word of Christ dwell in you richly in all wisdom, teaching and admonishing one another in psalms and hymns and spiritual songs, singing with grace in your hearts to the Lord. (Colossians 3:16).

Chapter 11
RADIO PREACHING

The radio offered more than just music. With tons of AM and FM stations to choose from, I listened to everything I could. When I first began to listen to all the preaching on the radio, I was inspired and awestruck. I loved to tune into programs like *Back to the Bible* with Woodrow Kroll, *Insight for Living* with Chuck Swindoll, and *Turning Point* with Dr. David Jeremiah. I so much appreciated learning how to apply the teaching of the Bible to my life. It was like attending church every day, several times a day! I loved it.

Focus on the Family with James Dobson was another program that instructed me in the practical side of Christianity. I learned so many things about myself and my rebelliousness. It was under the influence of these ministries that I learned that my ADHD was more likely a symptom of not receiving biblical discipline. I figured that if I stayed surrendered to God, I wouldn't need my medications so, even at the protest of the juvenile staff, I decided to refuse all my psychotropic drugs. I remember waking up the next day with a new vigor and clarity. It was like my brain put on glasses and everything came into focus. The fog lifted. I found myself able to grasp the principles and concepts of the Bible even quicker now.

But my favorite radio show was *Just Thinking* with Ravi Zacharias, who was an apologist teaching me *how* to think and see the reasons for my faith. Together with the program *Science, Scripture & Salvation*, *Just Thinking* taught me that we can lay a solid scientific foundation for the creation of the earth just thousands of years ago, not billions. The Bible has answers for the apparent age of the rocks and dinosaurs and explains what we observe today. I saw that the historical account of Jesus is verifiable and that we can trust the report of the resurrection of Jesus as much as we can trust anything. I was given more reasons for my faith.

One day, I decided to take a certain risk. While I was in the dayroom writing a letter, I realized that fifteen minutes was just not enough time to write everything I wanted to, not to mention being able to write down notes from the radio. So I sharpened the pencil and then broke the lead off of it. When no one was looking, I took the pencil lead and hid it in my waistband. When I got back to my cell I was so excited at all the things I could then do. On scrap pieces of paper or in the margins of my Bible and concordance, I wrote as much as I could. I would write a letter in small, light print to preserve my quarter-inch pencil as long as possible. When I got to the dayroom, I would re-write it more clearly, but not have to take time to figure out what I was going to say. I had to reload on lead about once or twice a week. Thankfully, I was never caught.

Though it was against the rules, I was glad to be able to write when I wanted to. As Mark Twain said, "The dullest pencil is better than the sharpest memory." I would take down prayer requests, write down lists of verses I wanted to memorize, and make notes of important thoughts. And I compiled a list of the programs I listened to on the radio. At one point I composed a weekday schedule:

5:00 Wake-up/*Unshackled* (89.1 FM)
    (Billy Graham on Sundays, 88.5 FM))

5:30 *Turning Point*/Breakfast

6:00 *Focus on the Family* (AM 1550)

7:00–9:15 Read the Bible

9:15 *Discover the Word* (89.1 FM)

9:30–10:00 Read book

10:00 *Insight for Living* (89.1 FM)

10:30 *Turning Point* (89.1 FM)

11:00 *In Touch* (89.1 FM)

11:30 *Back to the Bible* (89.1 FM)

12:00–1:15 Read the Bible

1:15 *Mark Hankens Ministries* (93.7 FM)

1:30 *Joyce Meyer Ministries* (93.7 FM)

2:00–4:30 Read the Bible
    (Sundays at 4:00 *Bible Answers Live* (AM 940))

4:30 *Truths that Transform* (AM 1100)

5:00 *Bible Talk* (AM 940)

5:30 Free time

6:00 *Adventures in Odyssey* (89.1 FM)

7:00 *Living Way* (88.5 FM)

7:30 *Family Life Today* (88.5 FM)

8:00 *Science, Scripture & Salvation* (88.5 FM)

8:30 *Insight for Living* (88.5 FM)

9:00 *Through the Bible* (89.1 FM)

9:30 *Just Thinking* (89.1 FM)

I was so thankful that hundreds of questions were now being answered, questions that were mostly simple. The whole Christian worldview was new to me. When I first started studying the Bible, I didn't know there was a difference between John the Baptist and John the apostle and revelator. I was so confused when I read stories of John after he had his head chopped off. I laughed when I realized they were two separate people.

I also had to learn that having humility didn't mean you had to look for ways to humiliate yourself. I had to learn that the Bible's book order was not chronological (which explained a lot). What was the Holy "Ghost"? I still thought we became angels when we died. I was learning the meaning of dozens of new and difficult words in my Bible (think propitiation, dissipation, fowlers and bucklers, sepulcher, sanctification, and predestination), not to mention the impossible-to-pronounce people and place names. Every stereotype about the Bible, Christians, and Jews had to be broken.

Most of the different preachers I listened to were what I would now call mainstream, espousing doctrines that fit within typical Protestant America. There were hellfire-and-brimstone preachers. There were preachers who were conversational and friendly in their sermons, fast preachers and slow preachers. No matter their style, I listened and learned.

This soaking went on for weeks. I thoroughly enjoyed every moment of it. However, every once in a while I started to hear my favorite ministers disagreeing with each other. It was subtle at first, but the closer I listened, the more I realized that not all these Bible teachers taught the same things. In fact, on some issues they completely and openly contradicted each other. I was disappointed to find out that not all Bible believers were on the same page.

One would say that once you are saved you are always saved and can never be lost; the other would say salvation is conditional on placing your faith in Him, repenting of your sins, and then abiding in Christ. One would say Jesus died only for those He knew would be saved; the other would say Jesus died for everyone. One would say we get baptized to be saved. The other would say saved people get baptized.

Was the gift of tongues for everyone, just for some, or had tongues ceased altogether? Was Jesus coming back before, during, or after the tribulation? Was tithing (a new word to me) just for the Jews, or should Christians tithe today? Related to that, what about the Ten Commandments? Were we obligated to keep the Law? Some preachers said "yes," others said "no," and still others said "just some of it." Could not these Bible scholars, who had been studying the Word for years, agree? How was I to know the truth about all of these doctrines? It was overwhelming.

I then understood why there were so many churches. Not everyone saw things from the same perspective; not all Bible students agreed on what the Bible said. I suppose it was only natural that people would disagree, but to disagree on something the Bible taught so clearly seemed odd. Some ministers, for example, believed and taught that the creation story from Genesis was just a story and was not scientifically accurate. They believed that God had used evolution to create mankind and that sin and death reigned for millennia before "Adam" came along. They taught that the Genesis flood was local and not worldwide as the Bible clearly stated.

I had to quickly come to a realization: there was an absolute truth and it could be understood. Not everyone could be right. If some taught that Jesus only rose from the dead in a spiritual sense, they were simply wrong. It sounded mean to say, but the alternative was to just agree that either it didn't matter or everyone was right. If everyone was right, then who was wrong? Was I wrong in my false religion? Was Satanism just another valid truth? The reasoning was flawed. It would have been an oxymoron to say that it was an absolute truth that there was no such thing as an absolute truth.

Frustrated at the confusion, I made a decision: I would study the Bible every spare minute I had (and I had a lot of them), to discover the truth. I would search out the Scriptures to see which ministry or church was teaching what the Bible taught. While I appreciated immensely the practical side of my Bible programs, it seriously bothered me that many would teach half-truths and whole lies. I acknowledged that I was new at this, and I realized my susceptibility to not understanding something correctly, but to explain that Jesus got into a fight with Satan in hell to win our salvation, or that we should call our ministers father when Jesus clearly said not to, just made no sense to me.

But how would I begin to study the Bible? How would I know what was truth? Enter the *Strong's Concordance*. What a gift from heaven! Thank you, Mom! This book was basically an alphabetical Bible that allowed me to look up any word and see every reference to it and what its definition was in Hebrew or Greek.

Each day I would hear new ideas on the radio or read something different in the many tracts, pamphlets, and magazines I was starting to get in the mail. I wrote every address I heard announced on the radio. I told them my situation and before long I had mail a couple of times a week. I then had tools to help me study my Bible and compare it with all I had been hearing and reading.

All I had to do was look up a subject like tithing, tribulation, or tongues, and read everything the Bible said about that subject. Suddenly, things grew to be crystal clear. I wondered why all Christians just didn't do this, because if they did, there wouldn't be the divisions that exist today with a different denomination on every corner. I searched out each and every question I had. I realized that the Bible didn't say a whole lot about some subjects, but with other topics the Word of God left me with no doubt. I studied holiness, faith, love, truth, grace, law, election, prophecy, jewelry, music, wine, patience, judgment, and so many more topics.

Chapter 12
MEANWHILE

The year 1999 began with my life in turmoil. Spiritually, I was drawing closer and closer to the Lord, but every other area of my life was falling apart. My lawyer had told me previously that I was facing about fifteen years in prison if I was certified as an adult, but now he informed me that the prosecution was seeking to enhance it to thirty years to life in the penitentiary. I had just found out that my victim, Keith, had mysteriously died in September. Was it my fault? Was it from what I did? No one had answers. My heart was in torment over my crime. I never even got to personally apologize to him for my unprovoked attack. I would forever bear the weight of my crime, which was only a small thing compared to what Keith had suffered. Oh, the anguish!

My attorney was going to try to convince the court to keep me as a juvenile, but he wasn't sure how successful it would be. If he succeeded, I would be free at twenty-one years old. They were going to be making the judgment based on my present mental faculties, not on how I was thinking at the time of the crime. And I had to admit that I was thinking more clearly now than at any time in my life. I was determined that whatever happened, I would be content.

During this time, I found out that my step-mom, Connie, had breast cancer and was fighting it with surgery and chemotherapy. Then my Dad's mom was diagnosed with lung cancer and given weeks to live. Grandma Ella May was the closest grandparent I had and I couldn't do anything or even be there. I received small updates from Dad in our ten-minute phone conversations about once a week or during our rare fifteen-minute visits. Dad lived over two hours away, and it was even further for my mom. While I knew my family cared for me and my future, I was beginning to care for them and their eternal future. I would assure them of my prayers and my love. I had told them the whole truth of my past and received nothing but their love and support. I had never felt as loved by them as I did now.

The juvenile center began making us attend school for a couple of hours a day during the week. Our teacher, Joe, was funny and very smart. He would work with us delinquents and encourage us in our academics. I was in the ninth grade when I gave up on school, so now I was trying to pick up where I left off. Joe taught us about politics, history, mathematics, and grammar. We had to memorize the bill of rights and summarize all the articles of the Constitution. We began writing journals and doing book reports. Though it was sometimes annoying, I enjoyed having the extra time out of the cell and being able to interact with others.

I also worked up the nerve to begin attending the weekly Sunday services. Darrell was from an Assembly of God church and he would bring students in from their associated college to minister to us and sing with us. I learned much from this and saw in them a genuine spirit of love. I really enjoyed the services and even started to share what I was learning. But I was mortified when Darrell asked me one day to close in prayer. I had never prayed in public before. I had seen him pick some of the other kids and never thought he would pick me. I was thankful everyone's head was bowed when my face turned red with embarrassment and my mind went blank. Somehow I made it through, but I have no idea what I said.

I tried to keep to a Bible reading plan so I stayed immersed in the truth. I wrote in my school journal for February 3, 1999:

> *I am now reading the New Testament once every month, along with reading the NT chapters one at a time to where I'll read it in six months with studying it in-depth. Also, I am reading the Old Testament six or seven chapters at a time to where I will finish it in six months. My future depends on my spiritual welfare and the knowledge of the Word.*

Somebody who caught wind of my conversion suggested that I let a youth minster visit me. His name was Sampson, just like in the Bible. Almost every Wednesday, he would stop by for a thirty-minute visit and share some precious things from God's Word. I appreciated his down-to-earth manner and his unconditional love for me. He was once allowed to bring in a life-sized crown of thorns and with it a powerful lesson of God's love for us. His weekly visits were encouraging and it was nice to have someone who could answer my questions. He was from the local Evangelical Free Church.

While the staff members of the juvenile faculty were mostly there to keep us from escaping and hurting each other, I discovered that they were human, too. Most, in fact, seemed genuinely concerned about us. During our short recreation periods, they would play checkers or ping-pong with us. Together we would play basketball or volleyball in the small gymnasium. But one staff member was different.

Tanya was a Christian. And although she was a deputy juvenile officer, she seemed to take a personal interest in our well-being. I could tell that being a supervisor was more than just a job for her; it was a ministry. If any of the kids seemed like a loner, she would go talk to them and encourage them. More importantly, she would listen. She carried a smile that was contagious, no matter how bad the day was going. And she didn't mind giving constructive criticism. I recall the first time she pulled me to the side and set me straight about trying to be other peoples' conscience—specifically referring to a fellow inmate, Tim, whom I thought I would set straight about a few things.

Only during weekdays for lunch did we get to eat in the cafeteria; all other times, we ate in our cells with only the peeling paint on the bricks for company. But Tanya would sit with us in the dining hall. She was always trying to eat healthy with her packed salads and vegetables. Gross! But her company was nice to have. She displayed the attitude and behavior a Christian was supposed to have; the attitude and behavior I knew I needed to have.

Chapter 13

DEATH AND HELL

I used to joke when people asked me where I was going: "To hell, if I don't change my ways." Of course, this was a strange answer for a person who didn't believe in a hell. *If it existed*, I thought, *we were in it*. Now as a Christian, I just expected that hell must exist and that Satan was in charge. The wicked were being tortured by the devil. Wasn't that what Christians believed? Satan ruled the "underworld," God ruled heaven, and the battleground was earth. It made sense to me. But was that what the Bible taught? Was the devil in charge of hell? That was certainly how Hollywood portrayed it and some preachers preached it. But what was truth?

I wondered about Keith. Was he a converted man? I didn't know. I knew that he did play an active part in his church. If he wasn't saved, I wondered if he was now in the torment of hell. Or if he was a true believer, was he now looking down on me with anger from heaven? What if he wanted revenge? Could he influence the angels to kill me? Either way, I was interested in his fate.

Bible Answers Live was a program I picked up on KSWN AM 940. One of the reasons I loved this program was because the callers would ask the same questions I had. The program was a live call-in radio show hosted by a couple of pastors, but I was catching the re-runs. It didn't matter to me; I couldn't call in anyway. When the questions were asked, I had to be fast with my tiny pencil lead, ready to take notes, because the Scripture references came like rapid fire from the hosts.

I hadn't been listening long when Pastor Doug Batchelor, the main host, was asked a question about what happens to us when we die. He said that the Bible teaches that we sleep in the graves until Jesus comes again. He said that Christians don't go straight to heaven after death. As I was hearing this, all my reasons for seeing this teaching as error immediately came to mind. If they are in the grave now, how could they be in heaven at the same time? He had to be wrong.

This was the first I had heard of this teaching about death. All of the other Bible teachers at least agreed that the dead go immediately to their reward. The caller objected, echoing my sentiments, saying that he thought the Bible taught that we go right to heaven or hell when we die. The pastor offered some proof texts, but I had already made up my mind about the subject. Too many "scholars" knew better than this preacher. Strangely, it made me mad that someone would try to make the Bible say such a thing. I had heard stories of near death experiences where a person would come back from heaven or hell and tell about it. Could they all be wrong?

Furthermore, he explained that after the wicked go to the lake of fire, they will be burned up into nothingness. He quoted a verse about the devil from Ezekiel saying that even he would cease to exist: "I will bring thee to ashes upon the earth in the sight of all them that behold thee. All they that know thee among the people shall be astonished at thee: thou shalt be a terror, and never shalt thou be any more" (Ezekiel 28:18, 19 KJV). I had been a servant of Satan, that great deceiver, and the thought that he wouldn't suffer forever disturbed me. Then he quoted Jesus' own words: "And do not fear those who kill the body but cannot kill the soul. But rather fear Him who is able to destroy both soul and body in hell" (Matthew 10:28). My head was spinning! He was suggesting that not only were the dead sleeping but that the wicked wouldn't suffer without end.

The same day on a different station I was able to hear another radio teacher talk about this very subject. He took a position opposite to that of Pastor Doug. He explained that we have eternal souls, and souls can't die. He shared several scriptures that seemed to support his position as well. He made a convincing case that the lost are already suffering in hell now and will continue to suffer forever. After this, I scribbled on a blank spot on the back of my calendar print-out:

Do the wicked eventually die out or burn up into nothing in the lake of fire? I believe no. Because in the same way the devil will be tormented "forever and ever" in the lake of fire and brimstone (Revelation 20:10), so does God live "forever and ever" (Revelation 10:6). Both forever and ever are #165 in the Greek dictionary in the Strong's Concordance.

I was decided. I rejected this idea of annihilationism as unbiblical. That is, until I read a book shortly after by Betty J. Eadie called *Embraced by the Light*. This book tells the story of Betty's near death experience in which she describes incredible details of her trip to heaven and what Jesus Himself and His guides taught her. In it she wrote, "I saw that death was actually a 'rebirth' into a greater life of understanding and knowledge that stretched forward and backward through time" (p. 40). *Does this mean I existed before I was conceived?* I asked myself. She went on, "When we 'die,' my guides said, we experience nothing more than a transition to another state. Our spirits slip from the body and move to a spiritual realm" (p. 83). This was very interesting.

Her story was compelling. It seemed authentic. She was calling me to love God and others, to pray and live in harmony with others. I felt privileged to have such a clear behind-the-scenes look into heaven and how God would have us live. She pulled the curtain on the mysteries of death and I was impressed. There were so many new concepts to think about, ideas to consider. But I came to a screeching halt when I read the next page:

> They [the guides] told me that it is important for us to acquire knowledge of the spirit while we are in the flesh. The more knowledge we acquire here, the further and faster we will progress there. Because of lack of knowledge or belief, some spirits are virtual prisoners of this earth. Some who die as atheists or those who have bonded to the world through greed, bodily appetites, or other earthly commitments find it difficult to move on, and they become earth-bound. They often lack the faith and power to reach for, or in some cases even to recognize, the energy and light that pulls us toward God. These spirits stay on the earth until they learn to accept the greater power around them and to let go of the world. When I was in the black mass before moving towards the light, I felt the presence of such lingering spirits. They reside there as long as they want to in its love and warmth, accepting its healing influence, but eventually they learn to move on to accept the greater warmth and security of God. (pp. 84, 85)

This couldn't be true! Atheists being converted after death? The Bible says, "And as it is appointed for men to die once, but after this the judgment" (Hebrews 9:27). And I found where Jesus clearly said that the evil would be punished: "Do not marvel at this; for the hour is coming in which all who are in the graves will hear His voice and come forth—those who have done good, to the resurrection of life, and those who have done evil, to the resurrection of condemnation" (John 5:28, 29). The resurrection? That's it! All of a sudden it dawned on me. Why had I not seen it before? The Bible talks so much about the resurrection.

It wasn't long before I had looked up every reference to "resurrection" in the Bible. I could no longer see the logic in going to heaven or hell immediately after death. There had to be a resurrection first. In John 11:24, it says that the resurrection will be at the last day. Paul preached the resurrection constantly and got in trouble for it (Acts 17:18–32; 23:6–9; 24:14–21). He even devoted a whole chapter to defending it (1 Corinthians 15). It ends with this promise: "Behold, I tell you a mystery: We shall not all sleep, but we shall all be changed—in a moment, in the twinkling of an eye, at the last trumpet. For the trumpet will sound, and the dead will be raised incorruptible, and we shall be changed. For this corruptible must put on incorruption, and this mortal must put on immortality" (1 Corinthians 15:51–53).

Yes, I could see it now—we all remain in our graves, to be *awakened* from our *sleep*. There were two resurrections (John 5:29; Acts 24:15; Revelation 20:5, 6), one for the righteous and one for the wicked. I chided myself for coming to my conclusions about death too hastily. I was ashamed that I let the deceptive book *Embraced by the Light* enchant me so much that I almost believed her story and the New Age "truths" she taught.

I had to take a fresh look at this whole thing. I appreciate that the Spirit of God would not let me settle into misunderstanding this subject. So I opened my Bible and concordance and read every verse in the Bible that used the words "forever," "death," "grave," "hell," "heaven," "sleep," "soul," and "spirit."

It was even clearer now. The dead are dead. Satan says they are not (Genesis 3:4). One of my favorite passages, 1 Thessalonians 4:15–18, made this more than clear:

> For this we say to you by the word of the Lord, that we who are alive and remain until the coming of the Lord will by no means precede those who are asleep. For the Lord Himself will

descend from heaven with a shout, with the voice of an archangel, and with the trumpet of God. And the dead in Christ will rise first. Then we who are alive and remain shall be caught up together with them in the clouds to meet the Lord in the air. And thus we shall always be with the Lord. Therefore comfort one another with these words.

Death is like an unconscious sleep; Jesus is coming from heaven to wake us up. But this doesn't happen until He returns a second time. According to this passage, we are to receive comfort from this truth. Before I believed, it was comforting to think that my Grandma Ella Mae who had recently passed away was "looking down from above." However, the resurrection truth is where true comfort can be found. (See Appendix 1 for more about what happens when we die).

I had learned a lot since I'd last listened to *Bible Answers Live*. It had taken me through some rough emotional and spiritual turmoil. But now I was excited to hear more. Sunday came and I tuned in again, hoping that Pastor Doug would address the topic of death once more. No one called about death, but someone had a question about "eternal fire" and asked him, "If hell burns out, like you said last week, how can the fire be eternal?" I guess I wasn't the only one with questions.

The pastor quoted the verse involved—Jude 7: "Even as Sodom and Gomorrah, and the cities about them in like manner, giving themselves over to fornication, and going after strange flesh, are set forth for an example, suffering the vengeance of eternal fire" (KJV). He said that to understand this verse you have to compare it with 2 Peter 2:6, which talks about the same thing: "And turning the cities of Sodom and Gomorrah into ashes condemned them with an overthrow, making them an ensample unto those that after should live ungodly" (KJV).

Basically, the results of the fire are eternal, not the fire itself. Eternal fire consumes eternally. To further make his point, he read Hebrews 6:2, where it mentions "eternal judgment." He said that God won't be judging the world throughout eternity, but His judgment is final. This really made sense to me.

But then Pastor Doug asked the caller a really important question, one which I had just learned about that week: "Do we have naturally immortal souls?" He then answered his own question by saying that there is nothing in the whole Bible that says we have immortal souls. He said that the Bible states just the opposite. I quickly wrote down

Job 4:17 and the passage in 1 Corinthians 15 which I had recently read. Both declare that we are mortal beings, he stated. He also quoted 1 Timothy 6:16 as saying that only God has immortality.

The caller objected, "But isn't it just the body that is mortal, not the soul?" I was wondering the same thing!

"Actually, the Bible says that souls can die. Ezekiel 18:20 tells us that 'the soul that sinneth, it shall die.' And we read again in Psalm 37 verse nine and on, 'For evildoers shall be cut off: but those that wait upon the Lord, they shall inherit the earth. For yet a little while, and the wicked shall not be: yea, thou shalt diligently consider his place, and it shall not be. ... But the wicked shall perish, and the enemies of the Lord shall be as the fat of lambs: they shall consume; into smoke shall they consume away (Psalm 37:9, 10, 20).'"

Then I began to hear the most profound reasoning I had ever heard. When God made man He made him to live forever on condition of eating from the Tree of Life. After their sin, they were removed from the garden and blocked from the Tree of Life. The reason given in Scripture was: "lest he put out his hand and take also of the tree of life, and eat, and live forever ... to guard the way to the tree of life" (Genesis 3:22, 24). If they ate from the tree as sinners, they would live forever as sinners. God didn't want that. He still offers immortality on condition of salvation from sin, but the wicked don't naturally have it. Therefore, they can't live forever in hell, because if they did, God would be giving them the same gift He gives the righteous. When I heard the following text read in this light, I saw this issue clear as day. Pastor Doug read Romans 6:23: "For the wages of sin is death; but the gift of God is eternal life through Jesus Christ our Lord" (KJV).

But hell isn't just a figment of some biblical imagination: it has a purpose. I learned that the purpose of the lake of fire, which will burn at the end of time, is not to please God, but to destroy sin and sinners once and for all. Hell will annihilate Satan and his followers forever. The universe will be clean and the promise of God will be fulfilled: "Then He who sat on the throne said, 'Behold, I make all things new'" (Revelation 21:5).

This idea was revolutionary for me. I had always had a twisted view of God. The satanic bible and other naysayers go to great lengths to paint God with a character that, as I then was beginning to see, is the very character of Satan himself. It is not God who is cruel and vindictive; He is not torturous or unfair. No, "God is love." "The Lord is very compassionate and merciful." "Great and marvelous are Your works, Lord God Almighty! Just and true are Your ways, O King of the saints!" (1 John 4:16; James 5:11; Revelation 15:3).

Will God judge the wicked for their wickedness? There is no doubt. Will hell one day burn? Surely. Thus, it became clear to me that God, being loving and just, will give to each as he deserves, exactly as Jesus said He would: "Behold, I am coming quickly, and My reward is with Me, to give to everyone according to his work" (Revelation 22:12).

It was refreshing to see God in this new light. I could certainly take joy in worshiping a God like that! (See Appendix 2 for more Scripture information about the nature of hell and the answer to my former objection.)

Chapter 14
GOD WANTED MY TIME

As with probably most young, new Christians in America, I read the Bible with assumptions and preconceived opinions about what it meant. I now credit my life-long indoctrination to the influences of Hollywood, family, and friends. I was not so gullible as to believe everything I saw on TV; however, when everyone spoke of something in one way without exception, how could I have been aware of other options?

Sometimes what is presumed to be truth is taught in this way. For example, I don't have to do research to know that New York is on the East Coast. Though I have never been there or met anyone from there, I just assume that everyone who has been is telling me the truth. Why would so many lie? Why doubt what everybody "knows" is true?

But the more I read my Bible, the more I realized that all the things I "knew" were true, were not necessarily so. For instance, I once believed that Adam and Eve ate an *apple* in the Garden of Eden, that all the animals went on the ark two by two, that men had one less rib than women, that Jesus was born on December 25, and that cherubs were little chubby babies with wings. Over time I learned that each one of these was a myth, misconception, or outright lie. Even learning about these many fallacies didn't prepare me to learn just how far the enemy of souls would go to deceive the world.

I had read the Ten Commandments many times and appreciated them very much. It was by the help of that law that I saw just how sinful I was and how much I needed a Savior. So it was strange for me to see my brothers and sisters in the faith disagreeing about it so strongly. The Christian news programs, talk radio, and even NPR (National Public Radio) were covering news about Judge Roy Moore, the "Ten Commandment Judge" from Alabama. He had the "Big Ten" positioned behind him right in the court room.

This sparked debates about prayer in school, abortion, euthanasia, and homosexuality. Some Christians were concerned that if you degraded the Ten Commandments, you would make way for many crimes to be committed without restraint. Others argued that the Ten Commandments were part of the old covenant and were done away with when Jesus died. Thus, God wasn't so picky about our behavior. Jesus focused on love, they declared, and downplayed the law. The judge and others said absolutely not, that the law was for all people for all time. Right was right and wrong was wrong.

My own studies revealed that Jesus taught that the law was *not* done away with. He said,

> Do not think that I came to destroy the Law or the Prophets. I did not come to destroy but to fulfill. For assuredly, I say to you, till heaven and earth pass away, one jot or one tittle will by no means pass from the law till all is fulfilled. Whoever therefore breaks one of the least of these commandments, and teaches men so, shall be called least in the kingdom of heaven; but whoever does and teaches them, he shall be called great in the kingdom of heaven. For I say to you, that unless your righteousness exceeds the righteousness of the scribes and Pharisees, you will by no means enter the kingdom of heaven. (Matthew 5:17–20)

I found a prophecy stating that Jesus was going to "magnify the law and make it honorable" (Isaiah 42:21 KJV). James said we were going to be judged by the standard of the law (James 2:12). Paul told us that the law was "holy and just and good" and was "spiritual" (Romans 7:12, 14). A few verses later, Paul wrote something very important about the law:

> What the law could not do in that it was weak through the flesh, God did by sending His own Son in the likeness of sinful flesh, on account of sin: He condemned sin in the flesh, that the righteous requirement of the law might be fulfilled in us who do not walk according to the flesh but according to the Spirit. (Romans 8:3, 4)

Wow! So the law was powerless to save. Only Jesus could do that. But He didn't just come to pay our death penalty; he came to show us just how terrible sin is and to show us how to do what He did: fulfill the law. So walking in the Spirit means obeying the commandments. No wonder He said, "If you love Me, keep My commandments" (John 14:15).

But I wanted to be a new-covenant Christian and not a legalist. These terms were being thrown around all over Christian radio. One was good, the other bad. I couldn't find "legalist" in the Bible, but I found out it was a label given to those who tried to keep the law to be saved. I knew no one could be saved by the law, but what was this new covenant that I was supposed to accept? Thankfully, it's never hard to find a Scripture with a *Strong's* at your side!

This is the covenant that I will make with them after those days, says the Lord: I will put My laws into their hearts, and in their minds I will write them," then He adds, "Their sins and their lawless deeds I will remember no more. (Hebrews 10:16, 17)

This was getting exciting! God wanted to take the commandments and put them right into my heart! Why would anyone object to that? As long as our motivation is to serve God out of a heart overflowing with love, then it can't be wrong to keep the law. But if we are doing it to gain God's favor, we essentially reject Jesus' sacrifice. I thought I was getting it.

In the arguments I was hearing about the law, the fourth commandment was raised a few times. This is the commandment that forbids work on the Sabbath day. Some were for it, some against. Most said it was on Sunday, but some were saying it was on Saturday, and a few even said every day was the Sabbath. One guy said he picked which days he made holy. It was an interesting topic to me. I was learning so much about the Bible and what God wanted me to do. I wanted to please God and do what He wanted. When I heard disagreements over a subject I was interested in, I went again to my trusty *Strong's* to sort it all out. When you read everything the Bible says about a subject, you can walk away with a clear sense of truth.

The Sabbath is on the opening pages of the Bible where God blessed and sanctified it (Genesis 2:2, 3). God used the Sabbath to test the Israelites concerning all of this law when He gave the miracle of manna (Exodus 16). It is the longest of the Ten Commandments (Exodus 20:8–11). After the exile, the Jews were getting in trouble for doing business on the Sabbath (Nehemiah 13). David wrote a Psalm especially for the Sabbath (Psalm 92). The gospel prophet, Isaiah, said much about it as well: blessings to those who keep it (56:2), that

Gentiles should keep it (56:1–7), more blessings (58:13, 14), and that we will be keeping it in the new heavens and new earth (66:22, 23). Ezekiel said it was a sign of sanctification (20:12, 20). Jesus taught that He is the Lord of the Sabbath day (Matthew 12:8), that we should pray that when the abomination of desolation happens we won't have to flee on the Sabbath (Matthew 24:20), that it was made for all mankind and not the other way around (Mark 2:27), and so much more!

Before I started hearing the debate about which day is holy, if any, I just assumed that when I read "Sabbath," it simply meant "Sunday." I admit I was a little confused by this when I read the gospel account of Jesus' resurrection:

> Now when the Sabbath was past, Mary Magdalene, Mary the mother of James, and Salome bought spices, that they might come and anoint Him. Very early in the morning, on the first day of the week, they came to the tomb when the sun had risen. ... Now when He rose early on the first day of the week, He appeared first to Mary Magdalene, out of whom He had cast seven demons. (Mark 16:1, 2, 9)

According to this passage, Jesus rose *on* the first day of the week, which was *after* the Sabbath had past. This means that Sunday couldn't be the Sabbath. Looking at my homemade calendar that I scribbled on the back of a writing pad I could see now that the seventh day is Saturday, not Sunday. How could I have missed it? Sunday was the first day of the week! Did God change the day He wants us to keep? Did He make another day holy? It took weeks of wrestling with my Bible, my concordance, and with what the preachers were saying before it all started to make sense.

It took me awhile, but after compiling all the evidence, it was clear that Sunday was not the Christian sabbath as many were saying. It was one of those take-for-granted things. We believed Sunday was the sabbath because we never heard anything different. We as humans tend to do what we've always done; believe what we've always believed. But even those who said Sunday was the new sabbath for Christians were saying that we don't have to keep it literally. This means that you can work as much as you want and not spend that special time with Jesus as He originally designed. So I learned that not just was the day wrong, but how they were keeping it was wrong too. I didn't want to be different, but I had to make a choice: keep God's commandment or a man-made tradition.

In my investigation of the Sabbath, I looked up all the relevant words in my concordance, finding the word "Sabbath" in about 140 places in the Bible. None of these speak of a change or a replacement day. I also discovered that the words "first day of the week" are used in eight different places in the New Testament. Examining each one in detail, I could not find even a hint of change in God's fourth commandment (Exodus 20:8–11).

A passage in Mark settled the issue for me once and for all. Jesus was again in trouble with the scribes and Pharisees. This time it was about a ritual washing of the hands and the disciples weren't doing it. When they asked Him why His disciples weren't keeping the "tradition of the elders," His response hit right at the heart of the issue. He said,

> "Well did Isaiah prophesy of you hypocrites, as it is written: 'This people honors Me with their lips, But their heart is far from Me. And in vain they worship Me, Teaching as doctrines the commandments of men.' For laying aside the commandment of God, you hold the tradition of men—the washing of pitchers and cups, and many other such things you do." He said to them, "All too well you reject the commandment of God, that you may keep your tradition. … Making the word of God of no effect through your tradition which you have handed down. And many such things you do." (Mark 7:6–9, 13)

In this account the religious leaders were attacking the fifth commandment about honoring your father and mother. By setting up a substitute law that caused them to disobey the commandment, they were, by Jesus' declaration, worshiping Him in vain. How much more, I realized, should I stay faithful to the Sabbath commandment? This commandment is about worship and spending time with my heavenly Father. If we changed anything about it and replaced it with a tradition, would we not be worshiping God in vain? In the Day of Judgment I didn't want to be found rejecting the commandments of God. "It is time for You to act, O LORD, for they have regarded your law as void" (Psalm 119:126).

It was around this time that Megan got locked up. She was my age. I saw her one morning across the day-room while everyone was lined up. Megan was in the same drug treatment program I was in before. We had been though all the same things together, the daily "grind," drug classes, the prison tour, and we both knew Keith very well. I was so embarrassed to see her. Of all the people in juvie, she would be the only one who knew what I did. I didn't know what to think. I was glad that only ten juveniles were allowed out at one time, and she was in the girls' wing, so I would rarely see her. But the emotion of it was building up within me.

The pressure on my mind and the resurgence of guilt forced me to call out for help. Later that night, after our recreation time, I asked to speak with Tanya, the Christian juvenile officer. She said that she had the time to listen to me, so I poured out my whole story to her. For the next hour or so, we shared back and forth. Her thoughts and wisdom taught me so much that night. I learned about calling out to God and finding strength from Him. I cried as I learned about forgiveness, trust in God, and how to deal with my uncertainty and the humiliation of my past. I believed that God could save me, but in my fragile faith, I kept being tempted to believe that my unworthiness would bar me from heaven.

Our thoughts gradually turned to more spiritual topics, and I asked her many questions. We talked until her shift was over at midnight, almost three hours!

As she would pass by my cell when doing her rounds, Tanya would sometimes stop by and encourage me with some word of Scripture. One of these times, she recited the entirety of Psalm 121, her favorite. I was amazed to think somebody could memorize so much! Sometimes she would ask me to read certain passages; other times she would ask me challenging questions just to make me think.

I appreciated her sincerity, her faith, and her encouragement. She began telling me about a book that meant a lot to her and that if she could get me a copy, she would. I was surprised how quickly it came, because the next day Tanya's book was in my box in the dayroom.

The name of the book was *The Great Controversy*. It was a very thick book with a black cover and large white letters spelling out the title. The more I read of this book, the more I coveted my cell time, as that was the only time I could read. In a couple of weeks, I devoured the whole thing; I couldn't put it down. It talked about the early church and how compromise began to enter into it. It showed that in the Dark Ages, even though God's people were persecuted, the true church has always kept the flame of truth burning. While precious truths were lost through pagan influences (as a former self-described pagan myself, I could see exactly what the author was saying), God had been leading His people back to a solely Scripture-based religion. By using the Protestant Reformation, God was able to call His people out of false worship. Many truths were restored, but His people hadn't yet come all the way out of Babylon (Revelation 18:4). There were still truths to learn (or re-learn). One of those truths was the Sabbath, the very thing I was just learning more about!

Throughout the book, the Sabbath was spoken of as a Christian institution that Satan hated because it was a sign of God's creative and redemptive power. This was new to me, but it made sense. I looked up the texts in the book and sure enough, it said just that in the Bible:

Therefore the children of Israel shall keep the Sabbath, to observe the Sabbath throughout their generations as a perpetual covenant. It is a sign between Me and the children of Israel forever; for in six days the LORD made the heavens and the earth, and on the seventh day He rested and was refreshed. (Exodus 31:16, 17)

Moreover I also gave them My Sabbaths, to be a sign between them and Me, that they might know that I am the LORD who sanctifies them. (Ezekiel 20:12)

The Sabbath was made for man, and not man for the Sabbath. Therefore the Son of Man is also Lord of the Sabbath. (Mark 2:27, 28)

The Great Controversy documented how Sunday began to be kept as a compromise with pagan Rome many years after the apostles died. It asserted that the Scriptures never issued a single command or counsel to keep any day holy other than the seventh day of the week. When Bibles were taken from the people, they lost the light of this truth; when they were again able to have their Bibles, a revival of truth began to burn.

I appreciated learning of the truth bearers of the past who were spoken of in Tanya's book. Their stories inspired me. They may not have understood everything in their time, but they sure stood for what they knew, even though it wasn't popular. Men like John Huss, Jerome, John Wycliffe, Zwingli, and my favorite, Martin Luther, taught me lessons of faith and dependence on God. I especially appreciated Luther's appeal before the Diet of Worms:

> I cannot submit my faith either to the pope or to the councils, because it is clear as the day that they have frequently erred and contradicted each other. Unless therefore I am convinced by the testimony of Scripture or by the clearest reasoning, unless I am persuaded by means of the passages I have quoted, and unless they thus render my conscience bound by the word of God, I cannot and I will not retract, for it is unsafe for a Christian to speak against his conscience. Here I stand, I can do no other; may God help me. Amen. (*The Great Controversy*, 160)

It challenged me to know my Bible for myself. I considered what it meant to have to answer for my beliefs from God's Word alone. I decided that I was going to follow Jesus, the Lord of the Sabbath, in keeping His day—the Lord's day—holy. I realized that this would not be a popular decision, but then again, when has it ever been popular to do the right thing? (See Appendix 3 for more information about the Sabbath).

Chapter 15

I BELIEVE

Scattered over several months, I received responses from the various churches I wrote. Almost all of them contained a creed or an "I believe..." statement. Near the top of most of the lists I would read something like, "We believe the Bible is our only source for truth and practice." Yet, strangely, what followed was a considerably divergent set of beliefs. They all agreed, for the most part, that their beliefs were based on the Bible, but then they disagreed about what the Bible actually taught.

Some beliefs were just plain strange. The Church of Christ believed that having instruments in church is a sin. The Church of God taught that sinners get a second chance after the millennium. The Pentecostals said that the only way to know that we have the Holy Spirit is if we speak in tongues (I had no idea what that meant). Lutherans baptized babies before they could even believe. The Unitarian Universalists taught that we will all be saved and nobody is really wrong, just different. Some taught that only the King James Version (KJV) was God's book and that the rest were inventions of the devil. We had no KJV Bibles available at my facility; instead, I used the New King James Version, the one my mother bought me. Would I be lost for using a different version? Some ministers taught that other books were authoritative such as the *New World Translation* from the Jehovah's Witnesses, *The Book of Mormon,* and *Science and Health with Key to the Scriptures* from the Christian Science religion.

With what I learned about death, hell, the Sabbath, and various other doctrines, I could see clearly that all of these faiths could not be right. If the Sabbath was not on Sunday, then every church that kept Sunday had to be taken off my list of possible true churches.

Immediately, the list got very small. There were but two churches in all of Springfield that professed to be Sabbath-keepers. They were the Seventh-day Adventist Church and the Church of God (Seventh Day).

I didn't really know anything about either of those churches. When I had first sent out my query letters to the churches, I had left those two out for some reason. I needed to know their perspective of the doctrines, so I finally wrote to them for their answers.

Chapter 16
PROVIDENCE AT WORK

I didn't realize at the time that Tanya was a Seventh-day Adventist Christian and that the book she had given me was a Seventh-day Adventist book. I did, however, read in the book about the Adventists of the nineteenth century. Were they the same people? I wasn't sure and the book didn't say. I also didn't realize that the *Bible Answers Live* radio program was run by members of the Seventh-day Adventist Church. What I did realize was that they were all saying essentially the same thing.

I eventually received the statement of beliefs from the Seventh-day Adventist Church and the Church of God (Seventh Day). They seemed extremely similar, but there were some apparent differences. The Seventh-day Adventists believed in a pre-Advent judgment, something I had never heard before. It had to do with a sanctuary in heaven where Jesus judges the righteous before He comes so as to give out rewards then. They taught about the Spirit of Prophecy, which immediately put me on guard. I had heard a lot about so-called prophets. They usually came on the radio about 1:00 in the morning saying some pretty strange stuff. Adventism seemed more structured and was a much larger denomination than the Church of God. Also, the latter group put great emphasis on the festivals of the Bible and taught that America and England were from the lost tribes of Israel. However, both groups said that Jesus' second coming would be personal, visible, and very soon.

This was a lot to take in. I still had much studying to do. By God's grace, I knew I was up to the task. In my studies, I especially guarded against one-sided arguments. I knew people would always place their own views in a favorable light, but when I saw deception or coercion being used, I immediately shied away. Both of these groups seemed fairly transparent. I knew that both churches could be wrong, but that both couldn't be right. God's providence continued to show itself.

At the same time, I was in the middle of taking about three or four Bible correspondence courses. One course was from Amazing Facts and another was called Discover from a ministry on the radio called Voice of Prophecy, both of which are Seventh-day Adventist. God's providence manifested itself when I figured out in a very short time that I was surrounded by Adventists. I wondered if God was trying to tell me something. If the Seventh-day Adventists were right, then I had some issues to resolve. I wasn't sure about so many things; I was still on guard.

One Sunday afternoon, while the staff was handing out our bologna sandwiches to take back to our cells, Tanya said to me in a kind of nonchalant way, "You know, the Bible says we shouldn't eat swine."

"What is swine?" I asked, because I didn't know.

"Pigs."

"Oh, but didn't God tell Peter it was alright to eat unclean things?"

"Just look it up and you'll see," she replied. "Remember, you have to read everything the Bible says about something."

I knew she was right about studying everything; I had yet to study this one out completely. I was skeptical; nevertheless, I went to work.

I found where Jesus did, in fact, say, "What God has cleansed you must not call common" (Acts 10:15). Reading the whole chapter again made me realize that He wasn't talking about animals at all, but about people. He was just using the unclean animals as a method for teaching stubborn Peter. The apostle would later say, in regard to the vision, "God has shown me that I should not call any man common or unclean" (Acts 10:28). It seemed that she was right, that God didn't want me eating unclean animals. Or at least this passage couldn't be used to prove that we can. I was excited about this new knowledge and planned to pass on the next pork product that was offered.

Jesus' death on the cross was not intended to cleanse animals of their unhealthiness, but humans of their sin. What sealed it for me was the realization that Peter hadn't, after all those years, eaten pork. If Jesus taught Him and the other apostles that it was now okay, why would he tell Jesus "No!" three times? (I noticed that he still didn't eat it even in Acts 10.) I decided right then and there that I was going to lay aside all pork products and trust that God knew what He was doing when He told His people not to eat unclean meats. "For the Lord God is a sun and shield; The Lord will give grace and glory; No good thing will He withhold from those who walk uprightly" (Psalm 84:11). (See Appendix 4 for more about unclean animals.)

The next Sunday when the church group came, I was excited to tell them about my new-found discovery. I knew that they were a little concerned about some of my new understandings, but I thought if I could show them what I had seen they would understand. We usually had several minutes after the service to fellowship and chat and so I shared what I had been learning. Two of the young theology students from the college seemed really concerned. They explained that I didn't understand the Bible as I should but that they had the perfect thing to help.

The following week, the same students brought me a special book, one of their college textbooks on hermeneutics. "Herme—what?" They told me that it just a fancy word describing how to study the Bible correctly. The name of the book was *Basic Bible Interpretation*, by Roy B. Zuck. I promised to read it and assured them that I only wanted to be faithful to God's Word.

It was pretty heavy reading, with lots of big, new words for me to learn, but overall it was one of the most practical books I had ever read. I knew I could only have it for a week so I condensed its 324 pages into small notes on three pieces of paper, front and back. This book taught me how to understand the Bible as it reads. My first lesson was to lay aside all my "ideas, opinions, and systems of our day" (p. 77) and let the Bible speak for itself. I learned to study the historical, grammatical, and syntactical context to aid in my understanding. Sometimes a phrase of the Bible is literal, sometimes figurative. Zuck said that knowing the difference demanded prayerful study, heavenly wisdom, and a knowledge of basic principles of interpretation. It was so good learning the difference between various figures of speech, similes, metaphors, parables, hyperboles, allegory, idioms, and parallelisms. I then applied them to what I had been learning.

I returned the book to the college students and informed them that I had applied the strict principles of interpretation of the Bible to the issues of pork-eating, Sabbath-keeping, death-sleeping, and hell-ending, allowing it to explain itself, just as the Bible said: "precept must be upon precept, precept upon precept, line upon line, line upon line, here a little, there a little" (Isaiah 28:10). I told them that instead of convincing me to give up these ideas, I was actually forced to embrace them more strictly. I had assurance in my beliefs and pled with them to consider what I was saying. I only wish I had done it with more tenderness and love and not with my attitude of self-satisfaction. I had much to learn about how to stay humble. I may have been right in my beliefs, but I was wrong in my arrogance.

Chapter 17
NOW AN ADULT

I changed from a juvenile to an adult in a single day: July 24, 1999. At least that was how the court saw me. After one year and twenty-four days, they considered me competent to stand trial as an adult. I woke up that morning as a kid, and by afternoon, I was thrust into an environment of thugs, killers, and rapists. I was expected to act the part of a man. I was sixteen years old.

Early that day, I was informed by the detention center administration that the paperwork for my certification had come through. I packed everything I owned into a little box: my Bible, my concordance, and a couple other books; my journals, letters, and lots of religious literature; and my Walkman radio. A sheriff's deputy came to the juvenile detention center, read me my rights, and re-arrested me; then I was escorted to the Greene County Jail. The only thing I got to keep was all my legal documents. Everything else was stored and was to be picked up by my family. It all happened so fast.

I was fingerprinted, photographed, stripped naked, and given a green jumpsuit, a fitting color for the Greene County Jail. The jail occupied four floors. Because I was only sixteen years old, they decided that I needed to be on the fourth floor where they held all the special cases. This included those on a Federal hold, people who were crazy (psychologically challenged), other young people, and those who were in protective custody. I was given a bedroll, a small tube of toothpaste, a toothbrush, and a bar of soap. I stood there at the airlock with the escorting officer ready to enter a pod with about twenty-five or so strangers. I took a deep breath. I entered the airlock. "Don't be nervous, don't be nervous," I kept telling myself. The steel, sliding door slammed behind me and the one in front of me began to open.

Jail was a holding place for men and women as they waited for their trial date or were serving a short sentence for some misdemeanor. If you were waiting for court, you could bond out of jail if you could afford it. My bond was set at $100,000. At that price, I would be staying there for a while. Many who were convicted of a felony were sent off to prison to serve for long stretches of time. Some people would just come on the weekends to work off their jail time.

I was the center of attention, of course, and everyone in the pod turned their heads to see the "new blood." I swallowed hard and went forward to my cell: 401. I got some nods and some smiles, but thankfully, no trouble. Phew. My new cellmate, Kenny, was in the cell writing a letter. He was being held for possession and possible manufacture of Methamphetamine (Meth) while he waited for his court date. He turned out to be a quiet guy who was kind enough to give me some much-appreciated sage advice about "doing time." In juvenile, there were no cellmates, no public showers, and no unsupervised time. In jail it was each man for himself—a watch-your-own-back environment.

If I remained in my cell and cowered, I might be considered weak and taken advantage of, so I put on the toughest face I could and did what was expected. I was tall for my age, about 5 feet 11 inches, but I could not grow even a single whisker on my face. No doubt, I looked young; I hoped the guys wouldn't notice.

So I ventured out. I didn't know what my fellow inmates were in for, but for some reason they were determined to know why I was there. I wasn't out of my cell for long when I was rudely interrogated by the others. If you were a "cho-mo," which is what they called a child molester, you were going to have a very rough time. I learned that in jail there is a pecking order, and if you had committed a crime against children, you were at the very bottom and considered the very scum of the earth. Your status was determined by what kind of crime you had committed. They seemed satisfied that I was in there for assault, though it seemed some doubted my story—that is, until a report on the 6:00 news showing my picture and telling my age and my charges: first degree assault and armed criminal action. There was a dayroom TV that was set by the guards and everyone there saw the mug shot from earlier that same day.

There were about twelve cells in my pod with two men in each cell. Some were in for bank robbery, some for domestic abuse, some for murder, and some for rape. We were not locked down except a few times a day when the officers would count us and also at night time. This meant that I could leave my cell and mingle with the other men. We could play cards or chess; we could talk or walk in circles around the three tables we had.

Even with my concern for my new environment, I was excited. For the first time, I could actually talk about my faith openly with others. I almost expected all the men to be just as excited about spiritual things as I was. I was disappointed to find only a couple of people who even read their Bibles. I had been a Christian for just about a year, and I had never officially witnessed for Jesus. Now was the time. If ever anyone needed a Savior from sin, it was we who were locked up for committing them, or so I thought. I didn't have much trouble convincing anyone that they were sinners. Most agreed that they were such. The problem was that they enjoyed it so much they didn't want to stop; they just didn't care. Why be saved from something that was fun and enjoyable? They could not see that "the end thereof are the ways of death" (Proverbs 14:12 KJV).

I eventually developed two nicknames, neither of which I liked. I was first pegged with the title "preacher" by some who said it belittlingly. My jail-house religion was annoying to them, not to mention my witnessing style was in much need of finesse and tact. Yet a few took interest in what I was saying. In fact, there was one or two who tried to convert me! I just wasn't Christian enough for them. The young Mormon man and the member of the Church of Christ were as excited about their faith as I was about mine—even though I was still figuring out what mine was exactly. But they would still call me *preacher*, even when I asked them not to.

Another name I received came from my curly hair. But my hair wasn't just curly. From the day I was locked up, I had never cut my hair. Instead of laying down, my hair would frizz out into a big 'fro. And it was big. Imagine a big ball of brown curls about twelve inches around a white face. They called me "big perm." It was an embarrassing name that I didn't like. I did my best to shake off the names by not responding to them. I met with some success.

As I was settling into my new environment, I received a new public defender and a court date. It seemed that I would be situated here for about a year before I had my day in court. I was content. This meant one more year of studying and learning, and one more year to pray and figure out God's purpose for my life. Jail offered me two special blessings: we had church services four or five times a week and our library was much larger than the one in juvie. I found a book there called *The Ministry of Healing*. This book was written by Ellen G. White, the same author as *The Great Controversy*! I'd had to send that book home when

I left juvie. If this new one blessed me as much as the first book, I was in for a treat.

And it proved to be just that. I got to see Jesus in action, ministering to others through healing and forgiving. I could see more clearly than ever Jesus' concern and compassion for humanity. In *Ministry of Healing*, I read these inspiring words:

Jesus was not satisfied to attract attention to Himself merely as a wonder-worker or as a healer of physical disease. He was seeking to draw men to Him as their Saviour. (p. 31)

In Christ, God has provided means for subduing every evil trait and resisting every temptation, however strong. But many feel that they lack faith, and therefore they remain away from Christ. Let these souls, in their helpless unworthiness, cast themselves upon the mercy of their compassionate Saviour. Look not to self, but to Christ. He who healed the sick and cast out demons when He walked among men is still the same mighty Redeemer. (p. 65)

Jesus knows the circumstances of every soul. The greater the sinner's guilt, the more he needs the Saviour. (p. 89)

I was falling deeper in love with Jesus! And I was learning so much about how to walk with Him. The book eventually turned to other practical things such as the connection between sin and disease, the laws of health, and the connection between what we eat and how we think. I learned what it meant that our body is the temple of the Holy Spirit and how dangerous it is to defile it (1 Corinthians 3:16, 17; 6:19, 20).

The knowledge that man is to be a temple for God, a habitation for the revealing of His glory, should be the highest incentive to the care and development of our physical powers. Fearfully and wonderfully has the Creator wrought in the human frame, and He bids us make it our study, understand its needs, and act our part in preserving it from harm and defilement. (p. 271)

God had my attention. I had already given up eating pork after the short study that Tanya prompted. But now I was seeing that the health laws of the Bible go much deeper than simply "do this" and "don't do that." God wanted my body to be preserved for health so He could use me in His service. I would either be glorifying or dishonoring God by what I ate or drank, or whatever I did (1 Corinthians 10:31). I decided that I wanted to glorify Him by my diet, whatever that meant. To this end, I was learning that God had an ideal:

> The diet appointed man in the beginning did not include animal food. Not till after the Flood, when every green thing on the earth had been destroyed, did man receive permission to eat flesh. (p. 311)

> Those who eat flesh are but eating grains and vegetables at second hand; for the animal receives from these things the nutrition that produces growth. The life that was in the grains and vegetables passes into the eater. We receive it by eating the flesh of the animal. How much better to get it direct, by eating the food that God provided for our use! (p. 313)

I was impressed by the wisdom and counsel this book gave. The message was Christ-centered and biblical. By the time I finished reading its pages, I had decided to stop eating flesh meat. I didn't give it up as a matter of right and wrong, but as a matter of health. If God gave our first parents a plant-based diet, put the Israelites in the wilderness on a flesh-free program, and blessed Daniel and his friends for their denial of the meat that the king ate and the wine that he drank, then surely there must be a blessing in it for me. This would be difficult, considering my present circumstances.

Of course, God cared about my health in more ways than just my diet. I learned about the Christian's duty to exercise, receive fresh air and sunlight, drink plenty of water, rest properly, and be temperate in all things. But the most important lesson on health I learned dealt with my relationship to my Creator. Trust. Facing the future I knew was coming could almost make me sick with worry and stress. I knew that trust in God would cure all the anxiety in the world. Easier said than done. God was calling for all of my heart. I yearned to give it to Him, and would search diligently to see what I yet held back. I struggled with self. I struggled with doubt and worry. I struggled with fear.

Once again the *Ministry of Healing* spoke to my heart.

Worry is blind and cannot discern the future; but Jesus sees the end from the beginning. In every difficulty He has His way prepared to bring relief. "No good thing will He withhold from them that walk uprightly." (Psalm 84:11)

Our heavenly Father has a thousand ways to provide for us of which we know nothing. Those who accept the one principle of making the service of God supreme, will find perplexities vanish and a plain path before their feet. (p. 481)

What powerful words! I could trust Him who knew my future. Nothing was going to take Him by surprise. Praise God for His promises: "Casting all your care upon Him, for He cares for you" (1 Peter 5:7). "For God has not given us a spirit of fear, but of power and of love and of a sound mind" because "there is no fear in love; but perfect love casts out fear" (2 Timothy 1:7; 1 John 4:18).

I was going to trust God in everything. By His grace I decided to stop eating meat, and, even if I had the opportunity, I also determined that I would never smoke, drink, or use drugs again. I even committed to never getting another tattoo. This was not my body but God's. I read in His owner's manual (the Bible) that He wanted to sanctify me completely, which included my spirit, soul, and body (mentally, spiritually, and physically) (see 1 Thessalonians 5:23). Jesus said to "love the Lord your God with all your heart, with all your soul, with all your mind, and with all your strength" (Mark 12:30), which was the first commandment. I couldn't see that I would be loving Him with all my mind if I was clouding part of it through drugs or alcohol, or that I would be loving Him with all my strength if I compromised it by not following His prescription for health in the Bible. I prayed for good health and trusted that as I followed His plan I would be protected from the diseases of my Egypt (jail). (See Exodus 15:26.)

So I decided not to eat meat if I could help it. But that didn't leave a whole lot else to eat. I wasn't allowed to give it away to other inmates in the jail cafeteria so I just threw my meat in the trash when I was done. I ventured to ask the staff if they had a vegetarian option. They told me that they did, but I would have to show a reason for getting it. I knew that the book *Ministry of Healing* was published by Adventists, so I wrote the pastor of the local Seventh-day Adventist church and asked him to write a letter for me saying that I had religious and health reasons for not eating meat. It took over a week, but finally they started providing me a vegetarian tray.

Only this meant that I couldn't go to the cafeteria any more, but had to receive my food in a Styrofoam tray and eat it in the pod (the dayroom of our cell-house) on a table separate from everyone else. I didn't like being singled out, but now at least I could have more food to eat than just a few vegetables.

Chapter 18
JAIL-HOUSE RELIGION

I didn't have a copy of God's Word for myself, so I wrote to the chaplain and asked for a Bible that I could use. He responded by sending me a simple hardback Bible from the Gideons, for which I was very grateful. The title page of the Bible said that it was the Authorized King James Version. It read very much like the New King James Version, and I quickly began to love its flow and style. Many of the preachers on the radio that I had been listening to for the past year used this version so I was familiar with many of the differences in translation. Now I could read it all the way through for myself.

It wasn't quite as easy to read as my NKJV, so I was forced to slow down to understand it. I found myself asking lots of questions about the meaning of some words. What were concupiscence, cogitation, and a collop? What did peradventure, pommels, and purloining mean? I had to learn that "fetching a compass" doesn't mean to go get a tool that points north, but to go in a circular route (see Acts 28:13). I learned all in their time, but it seemed slow going at first. Despite the difficulty, I could easily see why people cherished their King James Bible. I learned to cherish mine too.

About four or five times a week, religious services were held on the first floor of the jail and inmates were allowed to come from all the other pods to participate. As soon as I figured out about these meetings, I decided to go too. And I didn't miss a single one, except the Catholic service, that is. It was mostly Baptists and Assembly of God churches that came. It was at the Baptist services that I first began to sing the old hymns. While I was in juvenile detention, we were not allowed to make a single sound while in our cell. Even a quiet whistle would be detected by the microphone and would get you into trouble. So there was no singing except the contemporary songs at the Sunday meeting. I had heard the hymns on the radio, but now to join with the other saints in lifting our voices to the Creator was a delight I can't even express. I sang with gusto, though not with skill. I learned that I loved to sing!

The services weren't always the blessing I had hoped for. I was again faced with hearing various winds of doctrines. I chose not to argue for the most part, but I sometimes did ask questions. Some answers were to my satisfaction; many were not. I could see that most of the volunteers who came into the jail house would come because they genuinely cared about us. We were sinners in need of a Savior. Not all the people who came to the services were already Christian. Many needed to hear about the power of Christ. For that I was thankful and would give a hearty "amen" when a powerful point was made. But I discovered that many came in with an agenda.

One day, after about a month, an organization called the Church on the Rock came in. At first it was just a typical service calling us sinners to repentance. Some newer, get-you-moving songs were sung. As he preached, the minister went down the "Romans' Road" passages (Romans 3:23; 6:23; 10:9, 10; etc.). We sang some more. And the minister closed with a call to become a Christian. Nothing strange here.

Then something unusual happened. The leader asked everyone in the room (about twenty of us) to gather in a circle. He asked those who accepted Christ to raise their hands. Several hands went up.

With a sense of excitement, the preacher told us to all hold hands, which we did, and then he went on to explain what was about to happen. He told everyone that according to the Bible, when a person receives the Holy Spirit, he immediately begins to speak with an unknown tongue. He told us that this was called a prayer language and that it was the sign God gave His people to prove to them that they were "born of the Spirit." He said this very fast and with a building excitement. He then instructed us all to bow our heads and close our eyes.

He continued, "My friends, if you have accepted Christ as your Lord and Savior, I invite you to use the greatest gift God has given—your new prayer language. Some of you may need some help getting started, and God has instructed me to show you how to begin. Repeat after me."

He said a short phrase in some unintelligible-sounding gabble. Only one or two people repeated after him, and then only under their breaths.

"You're getting it!"

More incoherent words, but his example was longer this time. He waited for those to repeat it. A few more picked up on it.

"Come on now! That's it!"

The babbling came faster and faster. He was no longer waiting to hear others follow him. He seemed beside himself. Others too seemed lost to all things sensible. They began to yell things that sounded like nonsensical children's rhymes. By this time, I had broken from the circle and stood back with one or two other guys. Never in my life had I seen or heard such confusion and commotion.

The main leader fell down with a bang onto his back and began shaking as in a seizure. At first I was scared for him, thinking he was sick, but then, as others began doing it, I realized that this demonstration was not from a disease but from religious excitement. By this time almost everyone, besides the few of us standing back with wonder, was gyrating, jumping, falling, shouting, and babbling. The episode reminded me of a bunch of drunk and stoned head-bangers in a Slayer concert's mosh pit. Suffice it to say, I didn't want to return to that service again.

This was the first time I had encountered "the gift of tongues." I had heard one of my fellow inmates mention being "slain in the spirit," but I had no idea what that was, and not wanting to appear ignorant, I didn't ask. I had wondered, though. I guess this was it. In jail I didn't have a concordance or any reference materials, so my ability to research like before was hindered. Even my Bible was taken from me when I was booked into jail.

At first I thought I was missing out on something. I would pray that if this was of God, no matter how embarrassing, I wanted to have this gift of tongues. Other believers in the jail considered me a second-class Christian because, according to them, I didn't have the Acts 2 evidence. They told me they practiced this gift almost daily and that it proved that they had the Holy Spirit. But in watching their lives and seeing their fruit I didn't observe the evidence of the Spirit. So while they were outright sinning, and not even acting ashamed of it, they claimed they had a sign of God's approval. As long as they spoke in tongues, they were convinced that they were saved. They would be speaking in tongues up to the day they came to jail for some horrid crime. I had my doubts about this as a genuine manifestation of God's power, so I had to search deeper.

What did the Bible say? I read of "speaking of tongues" several times in the Bible, but I couldn't remember exactly what it said. I didn't have my concordance in the county jail, but I did have a lot of time on my hands, so I read the whole New Testament from beginning to end to see all the passages mentioning this phenomenon. I found that it said much more than I expected. God gave me much clarity on the subject. I learned that supernatural speaking in tongues is mentioned in only three books of the Bible: Mark (one time), Acts, and 1 Corinthians. I studied each passage in depth, comparing it with each of the others, and I discovered that the gift of tongues had nothing to do with a prayer language or with self-edifying as I had been told. Rather, it was a divine gift given to Christians to enable them to speak the native tongues (or languages) of foreigners so they could tell them the gospel of Jesus Christ. It could take years to learn a foreign language, but God gave them the language in seconds. This is what happened in Acts chapter two, and it allowed the gospel to be spread so very far so very fast.

I began to get the picture. God gave this gift to spread the gospel, but some were misusing the gift. They would use it and the only one that would be edified is the user, no one else. Paul had to rebuke them, so he wrote 1 Corinthians 14. So imagine a Brother Erastus who had the gift of tongues in Arabic to share among the Arabs. Let's say he was in the Corinthian Church one Sabbath and he wanted to share a word of encouragement or some teaching that God had showed him, but the problem was that no one in the whole church spoke Arabic (see verse 6). What was he to do? Many of the believers just shared anyway, even though no one had the "understanding."

What would Paul's counsel be to one such as Erastus? He said, "Let all things be done for edification. … But if there is no interpreter, let him keep silent in church, and let him speak to himself and to God." Otherwise, "you will be speaking into the air" (Verses 26, 28, 29).

Tongues were given to communicate to others, so if no communication could happen, it was best to be quiet. There is nothing in the entirety of Scripture that I found that implies that this gift is for everyone or that it is proof that one is saved. It seems the confusion was mostly arising out of the words "unknown" and "understanding." The KJV translators italicized the word "unknown," which showed that it was added and wasn't in the original manuscripts. It was supposed to show that what the speaker was saying was unknown to others, not to him. And similarly, the word "understanding" throughout the chapter was referring to the understanding of others, not the speaker. When I saw that this reading, consistently applied, harmonized with the whole, I was sure that it was the truth.

I felt bad for those who wanted me to experience their so-called gift. I wasn't sure what they were basing their experiences on, but it wasn't the Bible. The true "gift of tongues" can be understood and its aim is to edify; theirs met neither criteria. I determined that I would continue to "pray with the spirit, and I [would] pray with the understanding also" (1 Corinthians 14:15 KJV).

Some time later I shared what I had learned with my friend, Jim. He intimately tied his experience of "speaking in tongues" with his conversion and growth as a Christian. It was his assurance that he was going to heaven. After the Bible study, he sat back and thought for a moment and then said, "Wyatt, what you are showing me in the Bible is nearly tearing me in half." We prayed together and committed to following the truth, whatever that might be. (See Appendix 5 for more about the true gift of tongues).

My adventures in Greene County Jail included studies with Mormons, Native Americans, atheists, and members of many different denominations. I read the Qur'an. I saw firsthand demon-possessed men, fanatical religionists, and the most depressed souls in need of hope. I lived with murderers, rapists, thieves, tramps, homosexuals, drug addicts, and child molesters. Each had his own story. Each had need of a Savior. As did I.

My walk with Jesus became deeper in the Greene County Jail. I was discovering more and more what it meant to surrender all to Him. I loved Him and craved more than anything else to be His daily disciple. I wanted to witness for Him and work for Him. Jesus was all the world to me, my life, my joy, my all, as the hymn says.

I was also learning more about the Seventh-day Adventist Church. I went over and over their beliefs and literature and could see the harmony that existed between the teachings of this church and the Bible. I considered all the providences that were leading me to see that this church was God's church. Revelation 12:17 told me that God's last-day church would be keeping the commandments and would have the testimony of Jesus, which was the Spirit of Prophecy (See Revelation 14:12; 19:10; 22:14). This church met both of these criteria and was also in harmony with the other teachings of Scripture. So for the first time, here in county jail, I began to identify myself as a Seventh-day Adventist. I was not ashamed of where God had led me.

Chapter 19
BEING JUDGED

For ten long months, I sat in the county jail waiting for the final determination: where I would spend the next years of my life. I was under no illusion that I could very well spend a long time in prison. During my wait I had court hearing after court hearing. I had decided months earlier that I would no longer lie about my crime, but I still had to follow court proceedings. I decided I would not deny a thing. Some of my family and friends were urging me to take it to a trial and plead not guilty. But I *was* guilty.

So even when the prosecutor offered me a plea deal, I refused. She said she would take it easy on me and offer me ten years for the assault and three years for the armed criminal action to run consecutively. There was but one route for me—I would throw myself at the mercy of the court. This meant that I would confess my guilt before my judge and ask for mercy in his sentencing. I believed that God would allow only what was best for me.

This faith was unshakable. My attorney thought we could go to trial and maybe get some evidence thrown out. That would make our case easier. Furthermore, I could use my personal history of psychological problems to my advantage. I had been on every mind-altering drug thinkable in trying to treat all of my issues. The fact that I had overdosed on Adderall the day I committed my crime was something my lawyer wanted to use to my favor so I could plead not guilty. I refused to lie and after quoting some Scripture about my reasoning, I think he could see I wouldn't budge. He conceded but said that they could use that information to hopefully reduce the time I would serve.

I stood before my judge on January 18, 2000, more than nineteen months since being arrested, confessing to him that I was guilty of my crimes. Based on my own plea, I was found guilty of one count of first degree assault and one count of armed criminal action. The first count carried ten to thirty years or life in prison. The second carried three to thirty years or life. I was facing up to two life sentences. Judge Holden set a date for when I was to be sentenced.

Almost two months later, on March 3, 2000, the court would be seated for the last time to consider my case. It was the day to answer for the crimes I had so horribly committed. I was ready.

Mom and Mike, her husband, along with my dad and my Aunt Martha joined Sampson, my faithful brother and friend, to sit behind me and be there for me. Mom was going to get on the stand and testify for me and ask the judge to be merciful. This day, she would shed more tears than anyone else in the courtroom.

The proceedings began with the bailiff calling the court to order. The judge entered in his long black robes. I tried to read his face to receive an indication of mercy, but I couldn't see through his stoic expression. He went through some preliminaries and then the prosecutor began to make her case as to why he should throw the book at me. She argued that my attack was extremely unreasonable and unprovoked. She referenced my past rebellion, Satanism, violence, and anti-social personality traits. Then she referred back to several psychological tests that were performed while I was in detention and assured the court that I was mentally sound and competent, even at seventeen.

My victim's family was at the hearing too. The prosecutor wanted her to speak in the place of her deceased son. Mrs. Williams, my victim Keith's mother, stood up and spoke some of the hardest words I had ever heard or would ever hear. She told the court:

Your Honor, sir, there are a few points I would like to cover. From the news reports they say Keith's death was due to an unrelated illness. Keith suffered from epileptic seizures; that is true. But it was never documented in the autopsy report that his death was the result of an epileptic seizure.

Keith's health was greatly compromised due to several injuries he suffered from the knife attack, seven stab wounds, by Wyatt Allen. He was unable to sleep at night due to nightmares and flashbacks of the stabbing. His immune system was depleted due to the great loss of blood, six units, and suffering from a punctured lung from one of the knife blows, which caused him to be susceptible to two bouts of pneumonia and a string of respiratory infections, which he was still suffering from at the time of his death.

Had he not been stabbed and gone through all the emotions and physical trials that he did, I feel he would still be with us alive and well.

He helped so very many children and young people through the many programs which he served. He deserved so much better than this. This has affected all of us. Keith's siblings have suffered silently the terrible loss of their little brother. Nothing would ever be able to replace what we have lost, my son and their brother, Keith.

She was in tears and I was in tears by the time she sat down. What could I say? I had stolen the most precious gift one can have, their child. After she sat down, the district attorney told the judge that she didn't have anything more to say.

It was now my public defender's turn. He began by calling my mother to the stand. He asked her questions about my rough past and prior drug dependence. She answered the best she could, trying to say something on behalf of her boy. She couldn't hold back the tears when she was asked about the missing poster that she was forced to put up when I hadn't returned home for several days and when she talked about the abuse we had suffered as kids. Already her son had been away from home for almost two years. She would only get to see me every few months. She knew that I could be going away for much longer and this broke her heart. She wanted mercy for her son more than anyone.

After she stepped down, my lawyer made his case to the judge, asking for mercy and the least possible prison sentence. He referred back to my mental state and my medications as influences on my decision to attack Keith. He said, "We don't know why this happened, judge. But I think Mr. Allen is salvageable. I think he can be returned to society at some point, and if we do it correctly, he will be productive."

He pled my age at the time. He shook his head, "The combined offer is older than he is right now. They're entailing 18 years to a 17-year-old man, so that'd be double his life if he went away right now." He went on, "He's asking the Court to consider his youth, take a chance on this young man. I think he is salvageable." He took a deep breath and turned to me and asked if I wanted to say anything. My head was reeling as I spoke:

> Your Honor, I'm not any good at speeches. I mean, I messed up. I seriously messed up. I just ask for a second chance. I know I have problems I need help with. I'm just sorry, to you, to Keith's mom, and to Keith. I know you can punish me; I've done wrong, I deserve punishment. I want to lead a normal life someday. That's all I've got to say.

The judge was not ready to make a decision on the case. He called for a recess and told us all to meet again at 1:15, about an hour and a half from then. He returned and again we all arose to see him sit down. Without any further delay, he read off his decision:

> It will be the judgment and sentence of this Court on count one, the Class A felony of first degree assault, that I'll sentence you to thirteen years in the Department of Corrections. Probation will be denied.

> On count two, the felony of armed criminal action, I'm going to sentence you to seven years in the Department of Corrections consecutive to count one, the Class A felony of the first degree assault. Probation will be denied.

His gavel came down, and I was sent back to my cell. Twenty years. It was a lot, but I knew that I deserved every day. Just seeing and hearing Mrs. Williams and not her son that day, proved that. Add to that my mamma's tears, and I should never get out. But I received mercy. I deserved worse, but I didn't receive it. Praise God! A week later, I was on the bus bound for the penitentiary.

Chapter 20
THE BIG HOUSE

Before I left the county jail, I began to receive advice from all the guys who had already "been down." They said that the first thing to do when I got to prison was to get an extra toothbrush and sharpen it into a shank (knife) and keep it in the waist of my pants at all times. This was for my own protection, they said. Second, I was to find the biggest black guy in the chow hall with everyone around and try to knock him out with one hit or smash him over the head with a food tray. Even if I got beat up, this was to establish a reputation that I was fearless and not a "punk." They said this counsel especially applied to me considering I still couldn't grow any hair on my face. So here I was, "fresh meat" going to the "Big House."

The day came. Again I packed my belongings only getting to keep five of the pictures I had been sent, twenty stamps and envelopes, and my legal papers. I asked, and they even let me keep my Gideon's Bible. Everything else had to be picked up or thrown away. I was escorted downstairs and into a holding tank. My turn came to shackle up. First we were stripped, then we put on an ill-fitting orange jumpsuit, then came the leg irons, then the hand cuffs, then the belly chain, and after all that, a heavy chain that connected the belly chain to the leg irons. About forty of us shuffled along onto a large bus. I sat next to other convicts of every sort. For some this was a familiar ride, for others terror could be seen in their eyes. We had a three hour trip ahead of us before we would arrive at our next stop: prison.

Fulton Reception and Diagnostic Correctional Center (FRDCC), or just Fulton, as it was called, would be my home for the next thirty-two days until they figured out where to send me long-term. It was March 9, 2000. I was seventeen years old, just old enough to be placed into the general population. I was told that I had committed a man's *crime*, so I would do a man's *time*—in a man's prison. I had prayed. I had committed myself to God. I now moved forward in faith, claiming the promise that "Greater is He that is in you, than he that is in the world" (1 John 4:4 KJV).

I made out the prison as it came into view. Seeing all the razor wire told me more clearly that I was about to arrive at a prison than did the large department of corrections entry sign. We pulled up to security gate, waited for it to open, and then pulled forward. It closed behind us. This happened again at the second security gate and we were finally at our last stop. If the razor wire wasn't enough to put out of my mind the idea of escape, the surrounding death fence definitely was.

We exited the bus and entered a small waiting area where forty or so inmates were already waiting. Our chains were finally removed and I was able to rub my now red and tender wrists. But that was the least of my concerns. Two at a time we were forced to strip naked and go through a security procedure too shameful to relate. I felt violated in a thousand ways. Their concern was of convicts bringing in contraband. We then had to stand virtually naked in a different holding stall for what seemed like hours while the others were processed in the same humiliating way. We waited some more as the next stage of processing began.

We were ushered into a large shower area where we were sprayed on every inch of our body with cold bug spray and told to stand there for a few minutes before we could wash it off. I was embarrassed to be standing before all these men in my nakedness, trying to decide where to look. I figured that many of these guys were like me, uncomfortable and just trying to get through this nightmare. But there are always those few who poke fun and tease as their defense mechanism—and they were there that day too.

I was finally clean of the foul-smelling bug killer and was ushered to the place where I could get some clothes. I was issued three sets of gray uniforms (one of which I got to put on), two sheets, a pillowcase, and a small wool blanket. Out of a bin of assorted boots, I had to find a pair that matched and fit. The nurses, who were there the whole time, gave a short examination and asked some questions. Next, I had to sit in front of a large camera. I was surprised to see that other inmates were helping the guards with the processing. One of them asked me my name, then handed me a blackboard with the day's date and my new inmate number emblazed across it: *1036878*. He said with a smirk, "This is your new name. Now hold it to your chest while I take your shot." Minutes later, I had a pink prison ID card with my mug shot on the top left. I was officially a prisoner.

I was told to report to housing unit two, wherever that was. On the way to "Two House," as it was called, some of the inmates were saying that this was the house where everyone went with twenty years or more to serve. The housing unit was separated into four wings and was monitored by a guardroom located high in the center of the house. I was assigned to C-Wing. As I entered, the first thing I noticed was that the noise was deafening. Inmates were playing cards and talking around the tables in the wing. The one TV was blaring with only one or two people watching it. Inmates were beating on their cell doors and shouting to their neighbors through the open space underneath it. My new environment reeked of smoke and body odor. I could feel the tension in the air and found myself praying with every footstep.

The wing was designed to hold about fifty-two convicts in 24 cells on two levels. The cells had a bunk bed, a sink, a toilet, and a writing desk. The problem was that the prison was overcrowded and so extra bunks were placed in the wings between each cell increasing the capacity to about a hundred inmates per wing. I was assigned to a bunk in the wing. My bunk-mate had been there about one week and didn't look happy that his space was now to be shared. I had a footlocker (with no lock) to put all my stuff in and to help me jump to the top bunk. It was true that everyone in here was serving lots of time. My "bunky" said he would have to serve more time than I. But at least it wasn't as bad as our other neighbor nearby who had to do seven life sentences. I didn't ask why.

The first problem I had I smelled immediately. Smoking was allowed, and the staff didn't care who smoked and who didn't. Day and night for a month I was in that bunk breathing the polluted atmosphere. This prison was a dangerous place. People were beaten up for not getting off the phone when asked. Officers were often caught smuggling drugs into the facility in exchange for money paid on the outside. I chose not to go to recreation—a small fenced in patio with a basketball hoop—while at this prison in Fulton because of the horrible stories I was told about the trouble that lurked there. Some called it being scared; I called it being precautious. It wasn't fear; it was wisdom.

So what did I do instead? I read and studied; I watched and prayed. I minded my own business and wrote letters. Every once in a while I would get into a conversation. Since our bunks were stacked so closely together, people would talk to each other incessantly, which made for a terrible night's sleep, not to mention breathing smoke all night.

One day some Muslims engaged me in a discussion which quickly turned into a debate about whether or not Jesus was the Son of God. I was so frustrated that these people denied the very Being who had died in their stead. They even said that Jesus didn't die on the cross at all, but rather it was an illusion. What was the point of being religious and praying all the time if you couldn't accept the greatest gift ever given? I couldn't understand!

Interestingly, a non-believing neighbor, overhearing our heated conversation, suggested that I study the book of Proverbs to be better prepared to answer these Muslim people and to know how to talk with a calm attitude. Ouch. To be rebuked by an unbeliever hurt, but I took his advice and started again in Proverbs. Sure enough, I found that book to be chock-full of wisdom for conversations and discussions. Mostly I discovered that silence is often the best way to meet an argument, and if anything I should hold my peace until I've researched a topic. God cares about how I speak. (See Proverbs 10:19–21, 31, 32; 11:12, 13; 12:18, 25; 13:3; 15:1, 2, 4, 23, 26; 16:24; 17:27; 18:13, 21; 21:23; 22:11; 25:11, 15; 26:24, 25; 28:23.)

In the prison system inmates can shop at "the store." It is called the canteen or commissary. Each inmate has an account and is able to earn money. Most make $8.50 a month unless they don't have a GED or high school diploma; in that case they only make $7.50. With this money, they can buy stamps and paper, soap and toothpaste, bowls and plastic ware, and various food items. Thankfully they sold extra toilet paper at the prison, but unfortunately they also sold tobacco and rolling papers. The meager wages couldn't buy much, but some people had family who would send money to their accounts. I was blessed to be such a one.

My dad was able to send me some money every once in a while to get my basics and to help out with food. This is because we were only given about ten minutes to get our food tray, sit down, and eat. In reality, this was usually about five minutes because they started counting when the first people sat down. If we were the last in, we were almost being pushed out the door before we sat down. We had to eat fast if we wanted to eat. Another problem: every meal's main item was meat, and not just any meat; often it was unrecognizable meat. You didn't have to be a vegetarian to want to avoid those food items. So I was thankful that I could buy food from the commissary to supplement what I couldn't or wouldn't eat at the chow hall. Ramen soups, vegetable flavor, became my staple food, and not just mine, but everyone's.

The problem with having money, though, was that others could easily see that I had it, and if so inclined, they would try to take what it bought me. For this reason, I didn't buy much. I wanted to be as small a target as possible. Such were the conditions in Fulton.

As bad as it was, as a diagnostic center, where inmates are held until sent to a more permanent facility, it was relatively controlled and safe. Inmates were locked down the majority of the time in their cells or relegated to their bunk area, and when they did get out or get to move, it was only a few at a time and with very controlled movements. Just as I began to get accustomed to the routine of my new place, however, I was awakened early April 11 and told that I would be transferred, but I wasn't sure where. Missouri has about twenty-two prisons with roughly four or five maximum security prisons that hold people with as much time as I had. I found out that even with high security, there would still be maybe two or three staff on a yard where more than five or six hundred inmates roamed about at any given time. Some of these people would never go home. I had to reflect on my future yet again.

Before I left I made a commitment to God. I re-surrendered my heart to Him, knowing that without His aid I would never make it. I prayed, Lord "do not remember the sins of my youth, nor my transgressions; according to Your mercy remember me, for Your goodness' sake, O LORD" (Psalm 25:7). I held onto His promises like my life depended on them (and I know it did). I knew that "when a man's ways please the LORD, He makes even his enemies to be at peace with him" (Proverbs 16:7). And that, "You will keep him in perfect peace, whose mind is stayed on You, because he trusts in You" (Isaiah 26:3). God would be my protector. He would guide me. "I will instruct you and teach you in the way you should go; I will guide you with My eye" (Psalm 32:8).

Chapter 21
THE LAST STOP

I arrived at the Northeast Correctional Center (NECC) and went through a small orientation, not nearly as bad as the one in Fulton. Every one called this place Bowling Green, after the name of the small town it was near. This time, I was assigned to an actual cell in the R&O (Reception and Orientation) house. Our cells were larger than I had imagined they would be. Each cell had one metal bunk bed, a foot locker for each person, a stand-up locker that was split for two, and a metal desk. On the wall was a long shelf opposite the bunk beds. This is where those who could afford a TV and who were on the top bunk could put it and other odds and ends. The commode and sink were porcelain instead of metal, though the toilet didn't have a lid. This was the Hilton compared to juvenile hall and jail.

My first cellmate, who we called our "cellie," was quiet and new to prison himself. I asked dozens of questions about what to expect and about the normal routine here, but he didn't have a lot of answers for me. I thought I would have to venture out to find out what I needed, but help came to me—sort of.

I didn't know any of the rules yet, administrative or otherwise, but I soon found out that we were allowed to visit other cells with up to four inmates at a time inside. When my cellie was on the yard, I received a knock at my door and a face peeked in. "What's up, fish? You getting settled in?"

"Yep, just trying to figure out how to use a regular sheet as a fitted sheet."

"Oh, that's easy," he said. "Here, let me show you." He came in with his friend following behind him. "You take the sheet and completely wrap it under, like this, and just tie the corners together at the top and bottom." He did it to both ends. "See, as easy as that." With a three-inch mattress only about three feet wide, it worked pretty well.

"Hey, thanks, man." I said. "I'm Wyatt. As you can see, I've got a lot to learn."

He introduced himself as Eddie and said that he had been down for a while and was just transferred here along with his friend, Bruce. They were friendly and answered several of my questions like when was chow time, when did they have church services, when did we go to the store, and how long would I be in this house before being moved to a more permanent one? I appreciated their help. After Bruce had to go, Eddie let me in on several of the tactics and mind games that people play to take advantage of others. I could see that he was genuinely trying to help. I knew that there were predators in prison, those who prey on the weak. I had determined not to be weak, but I had also determined to avoid violence at all costs.

He told me about the bait and switch game. Someone gives you box of cakes, seeming to be nice. A day or two later, he comes to get his cakes back, but they have been eaten. The victim promises to repay, but the predator only wants the *same* box back. Not being able to pay exactly what he wants puts him in a dangerous debt that has to be paid other ways. So rule number one: don't take gifts and don't borrow. It made sense to me.

There were three things certain people wanted in prison: power, sex, and money, not much unlike the outside. To get it they resorted to violence, intimidation, and extortion. Eddie said that most people in here who wanted to be your friend really wanted something else, and to watch out. Watch out for the guy who wants to be your buddy and help you out, he warned; sometimes they will approach you and straight-out tell you that they will protect you for so much money and when you refuse to pay they will then threaten you themselves. I can't say his "prison lesson" set me at ease. He encouraged me to find some good tried and true friends that I could stay around for my own good. I didn't see at the time where he was leading with that.

He left out the other danger, the one that he himself was getting involved with and was subtly encouraging me to get mixed up with as well. This was the risk of joining a gang or a clique. There is always strength in numbers, but I realized almost too late that this comes at a cost.

Eddie would come over every once in a while and I would share some of my faith with him. He seemed to like what he was hearing. He introduced me to some of his friends on the yard. It was then that I noticed that many of them had something in common—shaved heads. I wasn't looking for trouble, but I didn't want to disrespect them either. As I was getting to know them, they seemed like normal people, just with dozens of tattoos, many of those being of swastikas or the SS lightning bolts. I didn't know anyone else. They encouraged me to work out in the prison gym and play handball. I started doing both. I felt comfortable around them and they weren't asking me to do anything crazy.

When I found opportunity, I shared my faith. They assured me that their group consisted of Bible believers too. They said this, yet I never saw any of their numbers go to any of the Christian services. When I asked them why I never saw them there, they told me that only the hypocrites went to church, and besides that, they refused to worship with other nationalities. They told me they weren't racist, but that they didn't believe in mixing nationalities. They called themselves Christian Identity.

I had never heard of that movement before. But I had already learned that just because the name "Christian" is attached didn't necessarily make it Christian. I wanted to know more. They brought me some literature that I had to promise not to get caught with. Apparently it was banned by the institution, but somehow they got it in. Truth has nothing to fear from investigation, so I figured that I could read it and apply what I called the Bible Berean test to it and see if it passed (Acts 17:11).

The religion was based on three main fundamental points. First, that salvation was based on belief *and* race. Second, that there were human races before Adam and Eve called "beasts." And third, that Caucasians or the White race of Europe and America are descendants of the lost ten tribes of Israel. They shared their books and pamphlets with Scripture references, but their case was not compelling. I knew that everyone descended from one man (Acts 17:26; 1 Corinthians 15:21, 22) and that we are saved by grace through faith and that who is in our family tree can't save us (Ephesians 2:8, 9; Matthew 3:9; John 8:33, 39; Romans 2:28, 29). They tried to justify White supremacy with the Bible. But their versions of creation, Israel, the Jews, and race were not at all biblical. I could see that though they were sincere about their beliefs, they were sincerely wrong.

They encouraged me to "click up" with them and said that I would be safe having them as friends. I declined their offers and started keeping more of a distance. This didn't make them happy. I had no intention of joining a gang or getting into fights to prove myself. I couldn't compromise my faith to have the advantages that being in a group provided.

Besides, I was beginning to make other friends, some of whom just happened to not have the same hue of skin that I had. I was amazed that some of these people were in prison. They may not have agreed with me on every doctrine, but their lives were upright and agreeable to the Scriptures. How did they ever end up in prison? I'd thought for so long that it was just me who was on fire for the Lord, so it brought great joy to me to find other Christians who were pressing "toward the goal for the prize of the upward call of God in Christ Jesus" (Philippians 3:14).

In juvie I was very limited in terms of where I could go and what I could say. In jail I had a cellmate and lived in a pod with many other people. We could interact and go to church services with other people from the jail, but our movement was still very limited. But now here, at my final stop, we had a lot more freedom. We had a yard that was open almost all day and as long as we didn't have a prison job or class, we could hang out in that yard with whomever we wanted. We had a gym with a basketball court, bleachers, and a weight room. There were horseshoe pits, a ball field, and a track. Prison was much different; it was like a college campus with a death fence around it. This freedom meant opportunity for fellowship and exercise and, unfortunately, it also meant an opportunity for trouble and danger.

I was moved to a more permanent cell and assigned to a job in the inmate canteen filling orders. I was only paid $7.50 a month because I didn't have my GED yet. It was hard work, but I was glad to be working and to have Sabbaths off. I was also enjoying the evening fellowship I was having with my new friends from church. We would meet on the yard or in the gym for Bible studies and prayer sessions. Sometimes there were up to ten or fifteen of us in a group studying this or that subject. I mostly sat and learned, but they encouraged me to speak up, and before long, I was leading out in these studies. We were all growing and learning.

But my previous "friends" were not so thrilled that I was seen with my black brothers. They talked to me about it and tried to reason with me, but my passion for God's Word overruled all. I told them that they were welcome to join us. About a week later, I was called to the sergeant's office and confronted by several white shirts (higher ranking guards) about a kite they had received. A kite is an internal letter sent to the staff and it is often used to anonymously snitch or report on other inmates. This kite said that if I kept hanging out with other races, I would be stabbed and found in a pool of my own blood. When they read the letter to me, they suggested that I check in for my own safety.

I had learned that there were four "jackets" (reputations) that no convict wants to get in the penitentiary. No one wants to be known as a snitch, a cho-mo, or a homosexual. And, just as important, no one wants to be considered a "check-in." Each of these could get you hurt, extorted, raped, or killed. I wasn't about to agree to that.

I told them no, and that I wasn't worried about it. They made me sign some waiver forms and sent me back to my house. But this only lasted a couple of days before another kite came in. Same thing. I again had to refuse administrative segregation. This was "the hole" and every one who checked in went there. I signed my papers and was on my way.

But when it happened a third and fourth time they'd had enough. One Friday, a corrections officer came to my cell and said, "Mr. Allen, pack your stuff. You're going to Ad-Seg for your own safety." I tried to explain to him that I'd sign a waiver, but he said it didn't matter, he had his orders. The hole meant I lost my job, lost the freedom of the yard, lost my phone privileges, and gained a "jacket" whether I liked it or not.

In the hole I was put into a cell with a man in his 40s who turned out to be the most racist man I had ever met. The irony! He ranted and raved the whole time I was there about his hatred for black people. But praise God, on Monday I was given a hearing to discuss why I was there. I told them I had no fear of anyone or any group. So they said, "Okay, if you will sign these waiver forms, then we'll let you out this afternoon." They put a pen in my hands that were cuffed behind my back and I joyfully scribbled my name the best I could on their forms.

Sure enough, that afternoon they placed me back in the general population. In fact, in a prison of 2000 inmates, I was assigned to a cell in the exact same housing unit and the same wing as before. This was a true blessing because, due to my short stint in the hole, people could see the truth that I wasn't a check-in, and so I was able to avoid the jacket I didn't want.

I wasn't sure if I was going to have any more problems over this issue or not, but I determined "to my own self be true." Besides, I found out that there was a kitchen worker who was a Seventh-day Adventist, and he was black. We met on the yard when we were both off of work.

Even though I hadn't had an opportunity to be baptized yet, I considered myself to be an Adventist too, and I was thrilled to meet another one for the first time (knowingly) in my life.

His name was Kenny. He was about fifty years old. I had a million questions for him and he did his best to answer them. He had grown up in Kansas City and lived a very rough life, which was evident from his scar-covered face. Kenny was serving fifteen years for burglary and assault. He was the meekest man I met in prison, and he was full of knowledge and wisdom. Before long, we became good friends.

Kenny had a Seventh-day Adventist background but had drifted from the church in his teens. However, his mother, Ruby, never gave up praying for him. Kenny now had a zeal for Jesus that attracted me. He wasn't like some of the other Christians who appeared to be playing the game. Apparently many people would get involved in the prison church because it was a safe way to be around other people. Kenny was different in a lot of ways. He enjoyed the old hymns, read his Bible constantly, didn't gamble or smoke, quietly shared his faith with others, and was also trying not to eat any meat.

Kenny told me what it was like to go to church "on the streets." He explained a lot about various historical happenings in the Adventist church. He showed me how our church had missionaries in almost every country of the world. He shared how Adventists ran over sixty publishing houses and over 5500 schools around the world. Kenny told me about the medical work our church did for the world, extending Christ's healing ministry to those who needed it, with over 400 hospitals, clinics, and lifestyle centers. I learned just how big our church was and how fast it was growing. Above all, he shared with me his excitement about Jesus' return. Together we studied, prayed, and sang. We would help each other be prepared for that day when the heavens will part as a scroll.

Chapter 22
LEARNING AND GROWING

My years at NECC proved very fruitful to my growth both spiritually and intellectually. After my first year there, I did not experience any more drama over my ignoring of the inmate rules about mixing colors. I respected everyone and it seemed I was beginning to be respected myself. I applied myself to bettering my environment and myself. I took the counsel of the Lord to Jeremiah personally:

> Thus says the LORD of hosts, the God of Israel, to all who were carried away captive: ... seek the peace of the city where I have caused you to be carried away captive, and pray to the LORD for it; for in its peace you will have peace. ... For thus says the LORD: After seventy years are completed at Babylon, I will visit you and perform My good word toward you, and cause you to return to this place. For I know the thoughts that I think toward you, says the LORD, thoughts of peace and not of evil, to give you a future and a hope. Then you will call upon Me and go and pray to Me, and I will listen to you. And you will seek Me and find Me, when you search for Me with all your heart. I will be found by you, says the LORD, and I will bring you back from your captivity; I will gather you from all the nations and from all the places where I have driven you, says the LORD, and I will bring you to the place from which I cause you to be carried away captive. (Jeremiah 29:4, 7, 10–14)

I was convinced that God had a plan for my life. It didn't consist of getting out, but of preparing myself while within prison walls. Time was the best gift that God ever gave and I had an abundance of it. I made it my motto: Don't serve time, make it serve you. I discovered that most criminals in prison can trace their crime to their first murderous act—that of killing time. I didn't want to be guilty of killing time or wasting it in any way. Paul, often a prisoner himself, asks,

> Were you called while a slave [prisoner]? Do not be concerned about it; but if you can be made free, rather use it. For he who is called in the Lord while a slave [prisoner] is the Lord's freedman. Likewise he who is called while free is Christ's slave [prisoner or bondman, *Darby's Translation*]. (1 Corinthians 7:21, 22)

I was the Lord's freedman. I felt free. Spiritually, I was free. I was free indeed.

I got a job in the kitchen working here and there. I wiped tables down, ran the trays and plastic ware through the dishwasher, and served behind the line. When an inmate came through the chow line, he would come to a little slot in the wall where a tray would be spit out, one after another. I was on the other side of that wall where I saw things that I wish I never had, things that made me hesitate to eat any of the prison food.

All kitchen workers lived in Eight House, so I was reassigned to the D Wing there, the same wing where Kenny happened to live. My new cellmate was a Wiccan who smoked and didn't use headphones on his TV. I needed to get out of there. I praise God for how He miraculously arranged for a cell move where I was able to move into Kenny's cell. People talked and rumors spread, but both of our characters put to rest any doubts about why we were celling together.

Bryan lived in the same wing. He was investigating the truths of the Scriptures for himself through the urging of Kenny, the same truths I had been learning over the past two years. Bryan was smart and articulate, an old Air Force man. Though he was twenty-one years my senior, we became fast friends. All three of us would study, pray, worship, and hang out together, both at work and on the yard. As strange as it looked to many, we would all jog together, though we couldn't keep up with Kenny. He kept going, mile after mile, while we would just continue to walk. Kenny encouraged us to stay fit and eat right.

Kenny showed true sorrow for sin and for the crimes he committed. Though he grew up in the Adventist Church he thought it right to be re-baptized to show his renewed dedication to the Lord. Bryan fell in love with Jesus and His truth. He hated the way he was and was ready to follow the Lord all the way. I had been aching for true baptism since my sincere but misguided self-attempt almost two years before. But there was just no way. We didn't have a pool or a pastor to perform the ordinance, but God provided.

I wrote to the Iowa-Missouri Conference which was made up of all of the Adventist churches in those two states. Before long, I received a letter from Elder Dan Kaffenburger, the pastor of the Jefferson City church. He wanted to get on my visiting list so he could visit me. I had never met somebody so well versed in the Scriptures. We talked as long as they would let us. On his second visit, he actually got to meet Kenny, who was visiting with his mom at the table next to us. But then he was reprimanded by the staff for talking with another inmate. If it happened again, our visit and his would be terminated. Our visits were such a blessing and Pastor Dan told me that he would do his best to make a way for the three of us to get baptized.

It was a couple of months later, but finally Pastor Dan received approval to enter the institution and baptize us in the newly constructed, small baptismal tank that the maintenance department had built and placed in the chapel. So on November 27, 2001, the three of us made our baptismal vows to God and were in turn buried in the waters of baptism. We outwardly demonstrated our death to sin, self, and Satan. We were raised into a new life in Christ. What a day of rejoicing! We were then members of the Jefferson City Seventh-day Adventist church. Hallelujah!

Months flew by. The routine of prison remained relatively the same. I left the kitchen to become a full-time student in the vo-tech department learning how to repair computers. I was so thankful for those opportunities. Bryan, who began working for the vo-tech department on a permanent basis, and I eventually became cell-mates. We were cellmates for several years. Every day, we would have morning devotions together. He taught me computer programming and how to speak American Sign Language. Because of his military past, he was orderly and disciplined, which I strove to emulate.

Besides becoming a Christian while incarcerated, I was also becoming an adult. Growing up in prison leaves most adolescent lessons unlearned. Virtually every influence around me tended toward the world and sin. People talked to each other rudely and aggressively and I still had to learn the difference between being aggressive and being assertive. If I copied the best of my society, I would still be completely dysfunctional. I appreciated some sanctified guidance.

How does one become a good time manager, money manager, and conflict solver? I realized that what was supposed to be common sense and basic knowledge to most people was unknown to me. Even worse, I didn't know what I didn't know! Thanks to Bryan and others like him, I was able to learn some of the more practical things of life. Wonder of wonders! To think I would go to prison to find such great positive influences for my life!

While examining my lifestyle and habits, I saw that there were things I wanted to improve. My diet was one such area. I had eliminated pork and most meats, but I was still eating some fish and chicken and the pastries with lots of sugar when they were served. Bryan and I were able to assist each other in this regard. Together we gave up all meat and animal products like eggs and milk. Though we knew that it wasn't necessarily sinful to eat those things, we knew, based on our research, that to continue to eat them would be presumptuously dangerous. Our health meant everything to us in prison. We also saw how our food affected us mentally and spiritually. It was amazing how such a simple diet helped to clear our minds to think straight. We often had to encourage each other when there was nothing to eat except beans—we ate plenty of beans. Even the meat substitute for breakfast was often beans!

Because of the lifestyle change, Bryan lost 45 pounds and got off his high-blood pressure medication. I actually gained a little weight as I got taller (I was still growing) and gained muscle. For years, we worked out together in the prison gym, trying to stay fit. Every Sabbath morning Bryan, Kenny, and I, and often several others would meet together on the yard or in the gym for fellowship and study. We did our best to "have church." We really wanted to have our own services like the Baptists, Muslims, and Catholics did, but our chaplain opposed the idea. He said they had enough "Christian" services and we didn't need another one. Though I persisted, he refused to budge.

Meanwhile, I was trying to find a minister from the outside to host an Adventist church service. Pastor Dan was already involved in prison ministries at two other prisons so he couldn't commit to holding services here, and though he tried, he couldn't find anyone willing to volunteer on a regular basis to visit Bowling Green. I wrote to more than ten churches within a couple hours drive and one wrote back. It was the Sunnydale Seventh-day Adventist Church in Centralia, almost an hour and a half away. Brother John Stone was a local elder there and was involved in prison ministries. He received approval to start meeting with us in the visiting room. It was very loud with dozens of visitors all around, but every other week the four of us would meet and learn and grow. It was over a year since we had been baptized.

Nevertheless, God was working. Chaplain Brown moved on and before long Chaplain Barnhart, a Baptist preacher who was very likeable, stepped in. I visited him one day and shared my request with him. When he found out that I was a Seventh-day Adventist, he told the story of how he was challenged by an Adventist neighbor. A storm kept the man from attending service on Sabbath, so he decided to visit Pastor Barnhart's church that Sunday. It just happened to be a day when he preached about hell.

After the service, the neighbor told him that the Bible didn't teach what he was preaching; he also told him that the dead were asleep and hell would consume the wicked completely and not burn without end. Barnhart disagreed, but the Adventist simply issued a challenge: if he would take a Bible and read it from front to back and highlight and examine everything the Bible said about this subject, then they would be in agreement when he was done. The chaplain was an intellectually honest man, so he took the challenge. Soon enough, he discovered that what his Adventist neighbor was saying was true. He said, "Wyatt, I like what your church is doing. In fact, if I wasn't a Baptist, I'd be an Adventist."

Barnhart told me that he would love to see an Adventist church in his chapel, but that we would have to show significant interest from the general population to justify having another service. We did our recruiting, and before long, several of us began meeting for our official Seventh-day Adventist services. Elder Stone came in faithfully every Sabbath and led out as we had a full hour and fifteen minutes to sing, pray, study, and worship the living God on the true Lord's Day! He started to bring us Sabbath school lessons and even found other volunteers, like Doug Graybill. Together they rotated week by week and made sure we could meet each Sabbath. Eventually such servants as Dan and Pricilla Jones and a retired pastor by the name of Albert Gerst gave their time to help us grow.

Here I was in prison and my life was as full as anyone would have hoped. Every day was an adventure and each experience brought lessons that would serve me throughout life. God's Word was becoming more and more real to me.

My friends and I knew the need to memorize the Bible. It is written, "Your word I have hidden in my heart, that I might not sin against You" (Psalm 119:11). Bryan and I had the opportunity to work out together a lot and we committed to take that time to memorize Scripture. Together we committed to memory the books of the Bible (backwards and forwards), the Ten Commandments, Psalm 23, 1 Corinthians 13 (the love chapter), Revelation 14:6–12, Psalm 119 (which took us a couple of months), and dozens more. We found many fun and innovative ways to hide the Word in our hearts. We figured that if we could recite the "love chapter" from memory with a heart rate of 170 beats per minute, we should be able to remember those precious principles when faced with temptation. Committing the Bible to memory has to be one of the very best ways of improving the spiritual life; at least that is my testimony.

Bryan also shared with me about his past experiences. He had been married and divorced more than once. And though he assured me that he was no expert on marriage, he did give me a lot of advice on what *not* to do. Coupled with the tons of counsel I'd received through books like *I Kissed Dating Goodbye*, *Messages to Young People*, and various church periodicals, I felt better prepared for when I would be released from prison. There was no doubt that I wanted to be married someday. But seeing all around me (and even in myself) the fruits of broken homes, I wanted to get it right.

I had never been in true love. I had only dreamed of what it would be like to be married. But I had to stay faithful to Jesus now and remain pure now if I hoped to be preserved for my future wife. There were plenty of trashy magazines in prison and lewd talk all around. To rise above such things without appearing as "holier than thou," I had to pray constantly and choose my company carefully. I resolved to keep my mind, as far as possible, completely undistracted (as Paul put it in 1 Corinthians 7:32, 33) and surrendered to the Lord. He began to arm me with the tools to remain an overcomer amidst the many temptations that I was sure to face after my release. His grace was, is, and always will be sufficient. I trusted that I would meet my "Rebekah" in His perfect timing (See Genesis 24).

Chapter 23
TESTED AND TRIED

Religious freedom is something very precious to Americans, even those locked up. For the most part, the prison system tries to honor the personal beliefs of its occupants. However, there is one thing that trumps all freedom in prison: the safety and security of the institution. Any freedom can be denied to protect the integrity of this place.

This translates into prison guards breaking up small Bible studies and prayer meetings. I was once forbidden by a sergeant from taking my Bible to the yard on Sabbaths. (It was eventually resolved). I was told that my desire for a plant-based diet was a personal choice and not a religious mandate and so I could get just a bean tray if I wanted. (Contrast this with the Muslims getting a special *halal* tray and the Jews getting a special kosher tray).

Prisoners had to work when they were told to work. Refusal could result in hole time. However, getting released from work on the Sabbath day was difficult. When I first got to Bowling Green, I told my case-worker that I wouldn't work on Sabbaths.

She tensed up and said, "You will if I make you."

"I would go to the hole first," I responded.

She stated matter-of-factly, "I can arrange that!" Then she sent me back to my cell.

I'm not sure why she didn't, but my work assignments always allowed me to rest on the Sabbath. Here I was so right and so wrong at the same time. Thankfully, I would learn how to find more tactful ways of requesting not to work on the Lord's Sabbath.

Zachariah studied with me almost daily for weeks. He could see the reason and truth in the three angels' messages of Revelation and decided to join the church. Finally, the day of his baptism came and he took his baptismal vows with all sincerity of heart. He didn't know it yet, but his faithfulness was soon to be tested. The very next Sabbath morning, he was scheduled to work on the yard picking up cigarette butts (the default prison job called captain's crew). His plan was to do what I had done in the past: go in and talk to the job supervisor and explain that Saturdays are the commanded rest day for Christians, sign out, and leave. The problem was that the sergeant in charge would hear none of it. Zach offered to work the next day or even the whole next week if the sergeant would just please give him Sabbaths off. He had more tact than I did and said "I *cannot* work on the Sabbath." Instead she commanded him, in no uncertain terms, to put on his work vest and walk around the yard and pick up the trash. She didn't want to hear "religious excuses" for not working. He decided to put on the vest and just walk around, but not pick up yard trash.

Bryan, Zachariah, and I did a lap or two around the outside track talking about spiritual things. But the sergeant came out and wanted to see inside the trash bucket that Zachariah was carrying. It was empty. She told him that if there was no trash in it by the next time he came around she would lock him up. What was he going to do? The whole next lap we walked slower and with much prayer. It was a solemn journey. None of us thought she was bluffing. He was convicted to do what his conscience said to do, so when she saw his empty bucket, she became outraged and demanded that he follow her to her office.

Bryan and I waited outside to see what would happen, and sure enough, when he came out of the building, his hands were cuffed behind his back and he was headed to medical for a routine check-up before going to the hole.

As he was going by us with his head down, looking discouraged, I told Zachariah that he had done the right thing and assured him of our prayers. About an hour later, Bryan and I were called to see the lieutenant in his office. For about ten minutes without stopping, he yelled and screamed at me for talking to Zachariah while he was on his way to One House, the hole. He said he could lock me up for inciting a riot. (What I said was construed to sound like a call to rebel from authority.) He spit out that he was tired of people coming to prison and "getting religion." To him I was hiding behind religion and using it as an excuse to be lazy. *A soft answer turns away wrath,* I kept saying to myself. So I softly explained that this was a fundamental belief of many Christians around the world and that we believed in obeying authority unless it conflicted with God's rules. I could hardly share before he cut me off with more profanity and anger.

In the end, he decided not to lock Bryan and me up, but to send us back to our cells for the rest of the day (called cell restriction). We both had to wear bright orange vests for the rest of the day. I asked about being able to attend the Adventist service that afternoon. He told us that he would allow us to, but we had to continue to wear the vests. When we were on the way to church, several people stopped us and asked why we had the vests on. It seemed strange to them to see us in trouble. We had the opportunity to share about Zach's stand for the Sabbath. We wore our vests without shame and almost as a badge of honor.

But it wasn't over yet. Later that night, the officer who escorted Zach to the hole wrote me a conduct violation for "creating a disturbance" since I was the one who had spoken up. A few days later, I had a hearing where I tried to explain the situation. But they didn't care. I was found guilty, cuffed, and sent to the hole for forty-one days. Zachariah would end up serving fourteen days in disciplinary segregation for his refusal to work; by God's providence, I spent about five of those with him in the same cell, where we were able to encourage one another.

The hole is a unique environment quite like my juvenile experience except we were never out of our cells except to take a shower every three days or so. The cells were bare and a Bible and writing supplies were the only possessions allowed. The attire was an ill-fitting hunter's-orange jumpsuit. The noise was a constant roar of talking, rapping, knocking, yelling, crying, and fighting; by constant I mean there may have been a break at between 3 and 5 in the morning, but that's it. So no restful sleep. Bowling Green didn't have air conditioning anyway, but normally we had a small fan to keep cool in the summer. But in One House there was no fan to help us keep cool, and no breeze to give relief. We would lie on our bunks and sweat in our hot cells, stinking because we wouldn't get a shower for another day. Our bird baths in the sink were all we had.

For exercise I would wait until the afternoon before showers, put my wool blanket on the floor, and jog in place and do calisthenics. My vegetarian option food that was shoved through my door three times a day was mostly three day old beans with fresh fruit about once a week. I won't tell you the details of how tobacco and lighters made it into the secure unit, but I had several cell-mates come and go who smoked unendingly.

But all was well, "for I have learned in whatever state I am, to be content" (Philippians 4:11). I surrendered it to God and held no bitterness to anyone. This was my time to catch up on reading the Bible. I was able to immerse myself in the fantastic stories and lessons that Jesus taught. I decided to "camp out in the gospels," as Chaplin Barnhart would say. God helped me to tune out all the distractions and share my faith with my "captive audience." But, thankfully, my six weeks came to an end.

As a result of this debacle, each Seventh-day Adventist was issued an official memo from the administration stating that they could have each Sabbath off. "And we know that all things work together for good to those who love God, to those who are the called according to His purpose" (Romans 8:28). Furthermore, after I was released from segregation, my conduct violation was completely expunged from my record because they said it was being doubly punished. Apparently the cell restriction with the vest was the first punishment. Looking back, I can see that these events were nothing compared to what the saints of old went through and what the remnant will yet go through if they stand faithful.

Persecution did not just come from security-minded staff members, but also from within. When I was released from the hole, Bryan already had a new cellmate, so I was moved to Three House with a man who was a known "daddy" on the yard. This older guy had "boys" that belonged to him. He assured me that he was not gay, but was only bisexual. I told him, "If you are having sex with other men you can call it what you want, but you are committing an abominable sin against God." He knew where I stood and that I would be looking to move out as soon as I could. And I did.

Ralph was a fellow Christian who lived on the lower block. He was an inmate preacher and led out in a couple of the services in the chapel. People respected him and it appeared that he was trying to live a Christian life. So we talked and thought we would be compatible cellmates. Neither of us smoked, we both didn't have a TV, we listened to our music with headphones, we liked it quiet, and we didn't like a lot of people in and out of the cell. He was clean and wasn't a homosexual. A perfect match. Or so I thought.

About two weeks after we started to cell together, I wanted to get ready for Sabbath and completely clean the cell.

"Hey, Ralph, do you know if you will be on the yard this afternoon around 2:00?"

"Why do you ask?"

I said, "Well, I was hoping to G.I. the cell before the Sabbath begins."

His face went hard and he said in disgust, "I will either be reading, sleeping, or writing."

"It would be less than an hour and I would be out of your way," I told him.

"If you want to clean the cell you can do it on another day!" Ralph snapped.

I left and went outside during the ten-minute movement at the top of the hour. I found Bryan and expressed my frustration as we walked around the track. At the top of the next hour, I saw Ralph come out of the house and decided to cut our walk short, thinking it would be for the best to clean the cell then.

It took me only about fifty minutes to wash our sink and toilet, scrub our floor and walls, and iron my Sabbath shirt. Ralph was gone all afternoon, but later when they closed the yard, when it was getting dark and the Sabbath was about to begin, he came in and said, "Wyatt, we have to talk."

Sitting down he said, "About this cleaning thing—I know it is your custom to get ready for *your* Sabbath, but I want you to know I will not accommodate you being under the law!" He went on to accuse me of being legalistic and having a self-righteous spirit. The more he admonished me, the angrier he became. As he was working himself into a frenzy, I just sat there and listened. My flesh wanted to respond in like manner, but the advice ran through my mind: "When passions are high, silence is golden." I was hoping it would calm him down, but the more silent I was, the more frustrated he seemed to become. His insults turned savage as he opened his mouth with curses and threats. I could see the satanic rage in him, the same spirit I'd had in my distant past.

"You think you are so holy, don't you, Wyatt? You say you want to follow the Bible, but you are a hypocrite just like the rest of them!" Raising his open hand in the air and clenching his teeth he asked with rage what I would do if he hit me. Would I turn the other cheek?

"By God's grace I will do what Jesus told me to do." I said confidently, sure he would not dare hit me. A bruise on me would place us both in the hole. He had too much to lose to risk that.

So I was stunned when his open hand came down upon my cheek. I was as shocked by the pain as I was that Ralph would sink so low. My cheek turned red hot, but not for a moment did I consider striking back. As I was wondering if I would get a black eye, he continued to curse and then started to throw things around the cell. He picked up and threw his foot locker toward me, but I picked up my feet just in time. I doubt I had ever prayed as earnestly as I had in the previous twenty minutes. Eventually he stormed out of the cell and slammed the steel door shut. In the quietness, I picked up the mess and thought about all that had just happened and hoped that when he returned he would be settled down. He reminded me of my dad when I was younger. He would often be apologetic after he had hit us kids.

Ralph returned when they shut the wing down to get ready for count time. I looked in the mirror and was glad to see that my face was a little red, but so far it had no swelling. We didn't speak for days after that, and though it took months, we eventually found new cellies. I do recall about six months later he approached me on the yard and thanked me for not telling anyone about the incident and hurting his influence. I had forgiven him and only hoped that one day he would himself embrace the truth about God's holy day.

After a series of miracles, I was able to move in with Adam, a brother just a little older than me. We were able to live together for almost three years in peace. Compatibility in who lives three feet above or below means everything. Adam was a true friend.

Chapter 24

REFLECTING

The pages of my calendar fell from the wall like the leaves of autumn. Days turned into weeks, weeks into months, and months into years. Though time often heals wounds, it could not bring Keith back from the grave. I had a burden to apologize to his mother. I wasn't even sure I had the right to ask her forgiveness but I had to try. I labored for weeks to write exactly what I wanted to say.

But even if she could get my letter, was I even allowed to send it to her? I talked to my IPO (Institutional Parole Office). She told me that if I contacted victim's services they might be able to make a way. So I wrote a letter to them to find out what to do. They said I could submit my letter to them and if it was approved, and if the victim wanted it, they would then forward it to her. So with a deep breath I dropped it through the outgoing mail slot. This is what I wrote:

August 12, 2004

Dear Ms. Williams,

While I hope this letter is appropriate, I understand if you wish to read no further. As I have thought time and again about what to say to you over the past five years, my mind has drawn a blank, only that my heart hurts with the knowledge of taking from a mother that which she holds most dear to herself. The following is just a feeble attempt to show how sorry I am, and how much I regret being so evil.

As I grow older (I am 21 years old now), I become more and more sick at the thought of my past and how I have caused so much hurt; especially how I have hurt you and your family.

Looking back, I see how repulsive my ways were. There is no excuse for my sin, only that I was wrong through and through.

Ms. Williams, I want you to know that even if I have to serve all my life in prison for what I did, it will never repay what I took away. Keith was a wonderful man (and you know that above all people), I only wish there were more like him, for then maybe the world wouldn't be so bad. In spite of all the good Keith did for me, I returned evil for good.

I don't expect or deserve mercy, pity, or forgiveness. No apologies can take away the pain, but please know that I am so, so sorry.

You will remember how before I was a member of the church of Satan, but I can now say that I am a Christian. While I cannot change my past but only suffer for it, my future will be different. I now live with the same purpose your son did—to serve others, to live to help. As he saw the best in people, even in a troubled kid like me, even so I hope to do. Keith loved sign language—something I didn't understand then. But now to repay just a drop in the ocean of my debt, I have learned sign language and help teach it to others. Maybe one day I can give back to society a part of what I helped take from it.

Again, what I did was deplorable and I am truly sorry. I have thoroughly repented of my ways and seek only to lessen your grief and sorrow for what I have done.

Sincerely,
Wyatt Allen

It was the hardest letter I'd ever written. And the toughest thing about it is that I never found out if she actually received it. I knew that when my parole hearing arrived in 2007, it was a possibility that she could be there. It usually is not good for the inmate when victims show up, but I had hope that I could apologize to her in person.

April 14, 2005 is a day I'll never forget. I was working in the chapel checking library books in and out. The chaplain was gone that day and Ms. Thomas, the secretary, was in charge. Toward the end of the afternoon, she received a phone call that left her noticeably shaken, but she didn't say anything. After I checked out the last book, I asked her what was wrong. Her eyes began to well up with tears and she said that I needed to report to my housing unit case worker after I wrapped everything up.

"What is it?" I asked her. "What happened?"

"I was told I couldn't say," she said with a look of anguish.

"Ms. Thomas, please, tell me. What happened? I won't tell them you told me. Please. Is it my family?"

She took a deep breath. "It was your dad." Now she was sobbing. "I'm so sorry, Wyatt. He...he had a heart attack. They found him dead this morning."

I had just talked to him a couple of days before. Everything seemed fine then. I remained as composed as I could. It was not too safe to shed tears in prison. It was considered a sign of weakness.

I thanked Ms. Thomas for giving me the news and made haste to get back to my house. It was a long walk, and along the way I recalled the last time I spoke with him. He told me about wanting to get up here and visit. We finished the call as we always did. We said we loved each other. For that I was thankful.

The housing unit staff with more matter-of-factness told me the same news Ms. Thomas had and asked me if I needed solitary confinement. Apparently some people lose it after a "death notice" and need to be locked up in the hole. I declined, but called my step-mom for a few minutes. Most of my dad's side of the family was there grieving over the sudden loss and I talked with several of them too. They shared how sorry they were for me and cried with me. The thought of never seeing my dad again or hearing his voice was overwhelming.

After I got off the phone I went to my cell, fell on my knees, and prayed. I poured out my heart to the Lord in many tears. I wept and wept until my eyes would not produce any more tears. I thought of all the missed opportunities of sharing the three angels' messages of Revelation 14. He knew what I believed, but I had never asked him to make a decision for Jesus. The truth about death and hell comforted me, but it was a small consolation in light of the fact that my dad, because of his failure to follow Jesus all the way, will miss out on the glories of the earth made new and the sweet presence of Jesus.

That day I reconsecrated myself to my Savior, committing to speak when He wanted me to speak and to share the everlasting gospel of

Jesus Christ with all who would hear. I wrote a letter to be read during his funeral service because I would not be allowed to attend. Time was short and tomorrow wasn't promised. I wanted everyone to know the precious assurance that being a Christ-follower brings.

Chapter 25

AN INSIDE JOB

Every inmate has to have a job unless they are medically incapable or are taking classes full time to earn their GED. I had met so many people behind bars who had no work ethic. But here they were mandated to work. They had played the welfare system and sold drugs. Many were lazy and others had grown up in rich homes. I discovered that the root of their criminal activity began in their attitude about work and their self-centered life. The prophet declared,

> Look, this was the iniquity of your sister Sodom: She and her daughter had pride, fullness of food, and abundance of idleness; neither did she strengthen the hand of the poor and needy. And they were haughty and committed abomination before Me; therefore I took them away as I saw fit. (Ezekiel 16:49, 50)

I worked the gamut in prison. I started on the yard-crew picking up cigarette butts and trash. Then I got to clean showers. I worked in our inmate canteen (we filled orders that were then processed through a window). I worked in the gym checking out recreation equipment and cleaning up. I also spent a year in food service cooking, wiping tables, cleaning trays, serving staff, and washing pots and pans. I worked on a power wash crew cleaning up bird-droppings around the prison. But of all my prison jobs, the one I enjoyed the most was working in the chapel.

One day I was talking to Chaplain Barnhart again when out of the blue he offered me a clerk position. I was almost twenty-one years old. I had been praying for that very thing; I wasn't learning a lot cleaning up bird feces. I immediately said "yes." Come to find out, earlier that morning he had fired both of his previous clerks for stealing. The joy of working in the chapel made "doing time" so much easier and enjoyable. I didn't know anything about computers except what I had learned in a six-week microcomputer repair class I took a few years before in the vo-tech department. But I would learn.

My duties consisted of checking out library books and tapes to other inmates and adding people to their religious service callouts. Knowing how to fix a broken computer and how to manage databases were completely different. Thankfully, Bryan, who worked full time for the vo-tech department, was able to come to the chapel when he was off work and help me learn what I needed to know. He tutored me in the different aspects of computing such as data entry, database management, and basic programming. Besides all the computer knowledge I was able to absorb, the various library books were at my disposal to read and study too. And did I ever study! I had some of the best reference materials at my fingertips such as lexicons, Bible dictionaries, biblical encyclopedias, history books, Christian biographies, biblical archeology texts, and more. Most of the time it was quiet in the chapel, but when it wasn't I could put on some headphones and listen to some good teaching. Amazingly, we had three evangelistic series on video by Adventist preachers: *Millennium of Prophecy* by Doug Batchelor, *Discoveries in Prophecy* by Mark Finley, and the *NeXt Millennium* seminar by *Dwight Nelson*. I watched each one several times.

As nice as the chapel was for studying, it had another asset to my Christian growth: the chaplain. Chaplain Barnhart or Chap, as I often called him, was in his 40s and had children about my age. He and I talked about everything imaginable. My experience working for him made me a better Christian and a better man. I could call him my mentor. He gave me good counsel on everything from finances to child rearing and discipleship to good business skills. He taught me that faithfulness is more important than results. He showed me that people are God's greatest concern, not policies. We had many things in common. As I shared before, he agrees with Adventists about the state of the dead and the non-immortality of the soul. He holds to the separation of Church and State as does the Seventh-day Adventist Church (and as all Baptists used to). The things we disagreed about we were able to discuss in a non-contentious way. Mostly our discussions were about practical matters. Being a gifted leader, he imparted to me much wisdom in how to interact with people. Working for him probably gave me the most real-world experience I've received anywhere.

We were only allowed to work in the chapel for one year at a time, so I rotated out to other prison jobs, mostly as a clerk in other departments. I worked for him about five different times over the years and loved it each time.

In February of 2009, I was offered a position in the vo-tech department, the same one where Bryan still worked. This department took donated old scrapped computers and fixed them up, then donated them to Missouri schools. I jumped at the offer knowing that having a marketable skill would assist me after my release. And so I went to vo-tech and built on what I had already been taught. I learned more in depth about various programming languages, networking, servers, computer repair, website design, and Microsoft Windows administration.

The penitentiary was my seminary and college. My aim was to become a productive citizen and I did not want to fail to take advantage of every opportunity. My diploma would be surviving this place in one piece. So many of my fellow convicts were becoming institutionalized; I saw the same people come back two, three, and even four times. They were serving life on the installment plan. This was not what I wanted. God forbid! I wanted to walk away free and *stay* free!

It appeared that God was blessing me like He did Joseph in Egypt. Unlike him, though, I deserved to be where I was. I was not, nor ever would be, worthy of God's love—but that is why it is called grace.

I have a theory that explains the passion of many precious souls in prison. Why is it that many in there have so much zeal for the Lord? My theory is based on a story that Jesus told Simon the Leper. A sinful woman had just come in and had begun to wash the Savior's feet. Simon thought to himself:

"This Man, if He were a prophet, would know who and what manner of woman this is who is touching Him, for she is a sinner."

And Jesus answered and said to him, "Simon, I have something to say to you."

So he said, "Teacher, say it."

"There was a certain creditor who had two debtors. One owed five hundred denarii, and the other fifty. And when they had nothing with which to repay, he freely forgave them both. Tell Me, therefore, which of them will love him more?"

Simon answered and said, "I suppose the one whom he forgave more."

And He said to him, "You have rightly judged. ... Therefore I say to you, her sins, which are many, are forgiven, for she loved much. But to whom little is forgiven, the same loves little." (Luke 7:39–43, 47)

My sins, which were many, have been forgiven by the sin-hating, sinner-loving Jesus. By His grace I would do anything for Him who rescued me from my life of destruction and misery. Why did He love me so? Why would He want a wretch like me with such a depraved past? It was because of who He is!

Chapter 26
THE BOARD

The board of probation and parole consists of seven members who together hold about 9,000 hearings a year. They determine whether or not a person who is eligible to be released is ready for the "outside" world. They base their decision on the seriousness of the crime, the time served, prison adjustment, and the recommendation of the institutional parole officer. My twenty-year sentence began to be calculated from when I was originally incarcerated in juvie. Unless I was granted parole, I would be in prison until my conditional release date of 2016, about eighteen years from the beginning. I was eligible for parole after serving 85% of my thirteen-year sentence, which was in 2009. Two years before that they gave me a parole hearing. My parole officer reviewed my case and told me that I hadn't served enough time yet, so she would recommend a "two-year setback," meaning that I would have another hearing in two years.

The parole hearing lasted only about ten minutes, during which they brought up every horrible thing I had ever done and gave me an opportunity to make a statement. None of my victim's family showed up. I didn't get to apologize in person as I had hoped. Three weeks later, as I expected, they told me I was denied parole and scheduled for a reconsideration hearing two years later. While they commended me for my progress, they thought that if they released me early, they would depreciate the seriousness of the crime I had committed.

When 2009 finally came, I was very excited because I was more hopeful that I would be released. My IPO was going to recommend a two-year out date this time, and based on my good conduct and programs completed, she thought it would be granted. But again I was denied. "Hope deferred makes the heart sick, But when the desire comes, it is a tree of life" (Proverbs 13:12). The Lord sustained me through my disappointment. Apparently He had a plan for me yet in prison. Were there still precious souls He wanted me to meet?

During this waiting time until 2011, I met another Adventist brother. His name was Roy; he and I became really good friends. We would study together, sometimes staying up until the morning hours investigating the truths of God's Word. His voice was golden and he would sing with me the old hymns and teach me Scripture songs. While Bryan and I were memorizing God's Word, I encouraged Roy to do the same. He said that he had tried to memorize large portions of the Bible, but that he didn't have a good memory. I challenged him to first admit that the mind God gave him was good and to not doubt God's power to help strengthen his memory. Second, I specifically challenged him to find large passages and hide them in his heart. He prayed and thought about it, then decided to accept my challenge. Before long, he had the first eleven chapters of Revelation memorized along with Isaiah 51–61. I realized I needed to challenge *myself* more!

While I waited for my next hearing, I continued to learn about computers and how to read and write Arabic, taught sign language, and held Bible studies regularly on the yard. My time was not wasted. I knew that I would not spend a day longer in prison than my God wanted me to. Some of my charismatic friends told me I didn't have enough faith and that was why I was denied, but I knew God was in charge. "God never leads His children otherwise than they would choose to be led, if they could see the end from the beginning, and discern the glory of the purpose which they are fulfilling as co-workers with Him" (*The Desire of Ages*, 224). The safest place was in the middle of God's will.

The governor signed a law that caused my minimum out date to be in June 2012, three years later than before but still only about sixteen months away. I was scheduled to have my next parole hearing in about four months when my custody level was dropped. I had gone from a level five inmate to level four when I had seven years before my "out date." Now, in 2011, I was five years away from my scheduled release in 2016 and so I was dropped to a level three. Bowling Green was an institution for levels four and five; thus I had to be transferred to a lower security prison. They chose Pacific (officially called Missouri Eastern Correctional Center) for me to stay.

It was like a night and day difference at this new "camp." We were only locked down four times a day for count and at lights out. Movement was not as controlled. The gym had much better weights and work out equipment. There were two ball fields and plenty of places to play handball and racquetball. At Bowling Green, I had seen a man get stabbed to death and many others cut and beat to a pulp. I had seen racial wars and experienced long-term lock downs. There were guys named Sabrina and Candy with homosexuality everywhere. But in my new residence, I saw only a few fist fights. Most of the people were going home soon and they didn't want to mess that up. Even though I was still in prison, I felt one step closer to home and slightly freer. My second day, I was called to be the clerk over all the food service, then the food service warehouse called and wanted me to be the clerk there. Apparently someone had read my file and I was happy they had.

The year 2018 was a long way away and I really prayed hard and searched my heart to see if there was anything hindering the Lord's blessing. This hearing lasted almost thirty minutes and I was allowed to share my faith and my plans for the future. I had been afraid to mention it before because of how many people they must see that use "religion" to plead for mercy. I figured that this time they needed to know I had a church family on the outside that would be happy to help. The Sunnydale Church, which has so many prison ministry volunteers, had agreed to help me get a start at life.

I waited only two weeks before I received their answer: I would serve the absolute minimum and be released in exactly one year. I was going home in June 2012!

I was shipped off again. This time, because I had only one year remaining, I was sent to a work release program at Farmington Correctional Center. After I arrived, they said I couldn't be let out of the institution because of my dangerous felony, but that I qualified to work in the laundry department and live in thirty house. Thirty house was different than anything I had ever seen before. I was in a twelve-man cell with no locks on the doors. Ten of them smoked cigarettes, but I was almost home!

At the laundry department about 150 guys shook out, washed, dried, and folded dirty (the worst imaginable) hospital laundry seven days a week. I had no problem getting Sabbaths off and was even promoted to teaching a computer literacy class for the other inmates. At this job, I made $0.72 an hour and was able to save up some money for after my release.

Time passed quickly there as I looked forward to my release. Eventually I had ninety-nine days and a wake-up. Then twenty-nine. Then two. It was becoming real to me. My "home plan" was all arranged. The Sunnydale church had a furnished apartment waiting for me. Another church member who owned a used car business was fixing up a car just for me! I didn't know what I would do for work yet, but I knew God would provide.

The day before I was to be released I went on my merry-go-round. That is where I merrily went around the prison turning in all my state-issued clothes, packing all my property into a box or two, and visiting medical for one last check-up. I went around to all my friends and shook their hands and gave them hugs (completely acceptable in prison for Christians). I gave them parting advice and they gave me parting advice. I would be leaving in the morning.

Chapter 27

AND A WAKE UP

The night before my liberation, I slept surprisingly well. I woke up at about 5:00 AM on June 19, 2012, and spent some precious time with Jesus. The story of the Bible left behind on the bunk when a convict gets out is a classic tale in prison. I knew it would not be true for me. God's Word had sustained me all through my journey and He had never failed me. Why should I now forsake Him when I need Him most? I would not leave my Bible or my faith behind. Freedom does not come without its trials and I could not face them without God's guidance and His Spirit. God promised:

A bruised reed He will not break, and smoking flax He will not quench; He will bring forth justice for truth. He will not fail nor be discouraged, Till He has established justice in the earth; And the coastlands shall wait for His law." Thus says God the LORD, Who created the heavens and stretched them out, Who spread forth the earth and that which comes from it, Who gives breath to the people on it, And spirit to those who walk on it: "I, the LORD, have called You in righteousness, And will hold Your hand; I will keep You and give You as a covenant to the people, As a light to the Gentiles, To open blind eyes, To bring out prisoners from the prison, Those who sit in darkness from the prison house." (Isaiah 42:3–7)

When count-time rolled around at 6:00, I was dressed and ready to go. I went and ate my last prison meal. I wouldn't miss the food. I wouldn't miss the incessant pat downs and invasive shakedowns. I wouldn't miss having to strip down or lock down at some officer's whim. I wouldn't miss the vulgarity always in my ears and the hate in others' eyes. I wouldn't miss the bad attitudes, the rampant homosexuality, racism, and oppression. I wouldn't miss prison at all.

My cellmates had mostly all left for work and I waited around to be called to the administration building. My excitement was building and building, and then over the intercom system I heard it repeated twice: "Offender Allen report to the administration building." It was 8:00.

I picked up my few belongings from the property room, waited for some others who were accompanying us, and made my way to the "outside" with them. Together we went through several stages of security before I could, at last, see my mom and sister, Nicole, waiting on me. A saint from the church had brought them to pick me up. We hugged for longer than three seconds (the limit at visits). I was as happy as a person could possibly be. I was free. I was free!

We drove almost three hours to my new apartment just north of Columbia, Missouri. We talked the whole way. My eyes watched all the passing trees and absorbed the beautiful sights of nature. Dustin, my brother, though he couldn't come, had bought me a brand-new smartphone and put me on his phone plan. I barely had it out of the box when I started receiving calls from my family congratulating me on my release. I had kept up with technology and what these phones could do, but I had a lot to learn. When I put the phone to my face to hear the person on the other end, I stuck it to my cheek and kept saying, "Hello…hello." I didn't know how to hold it. Nicole had to show me how to put it to my ear in just the right way.

That evening my brother Joe and his girlfriend had prepared a very special vegetarian meal for me. Nicole joined us, and for the first time in years I was able to eat a dinner in peace without the rush and noise of a prison chow hall. I'll never forget that lentil soup and bowl of fresh fruit salad.

I felt so unworthy of all the love bestowed upon me by my family and my church. In fact, I *was* unworthy, but that is why I consider myself a child of grace. At every critical point in my life, I have received abundant grace from God. I have not been treated as I deserved, but rather as Christ deserved. It reminded me of the story of Paul and Onesimus in the Bible.

Paul was a prisoner "doing time" for his ministry for Christ. He got a new cellmate one day by the name of Onesimus who was a fugitive slave from Colossae who had wronged his master, Philemon, a Christ-follower. The aged apostle shared about what a wonderful friend he had found in Jesus. Paul preached the gospel to him and as Onesimus heard the words of life, he confessed his sins and surrendered to Christ.

I can see Onesimus soaking up, every word of counsel, every admonition, from the lips of his fellow prisoner. But the day of his release was coming. Paul had been watching him. He could see the fruits of true conversion. He took note of Onesimus' zeal and knew that he had a work to do. The same energy Onesimus had used to serve self and Satan he could now put into the service of his new Master. Paul sent him back to Philemon to ask his forgiveness and become a "profitable" servant.

Paul sent Onesimus with a letter to give to Philemon in which he said: "I am sending him back. You therefore receive him, that is, my own heart." He knew that God works all things together for good and suggested that "perhaps he departed for a while for this purpose, that you might receive him forever, no longer as a slave but more than a slave—a beloved brother, especially to me but how much more to you, both in the flesh and in the Lord" (Philemon 1:12, 15, 16). Imagine going back to work for the same man he had wronged. Would he be accepted? Would he be trusted?

Paul (a.k.a. Saul) had been in Onesimus' shoes. He "was former-ly a blasphemer, a persecutor, and an insolent man." And so after his conversion, "when Saul had come to Jerusalem, he tried to join the disciples; but they were all afraid of him, and did not believe that he was a disciple" (1 Timothy 1:13; Acts 9:26).

So Paul vouched for his new friend and brother. He promised to hold himself responsible for whatever Onesimus had cost Philemon. He asked Philemon to receive back the repentant slave even "as you would me" (Philemon 1:17). What love! What compassion! What con-fidence in this young man!

I felt like Onesimus, returning to a society from which I had taken so much. But here were those who, like the apostle Paul, had sacrificed so much to see me prosper. It was humbling to see Jesus so clearly re-flected in His people. How could I say thanks enough?

Chapter 28
I'M OUT!

I had been warned for years not to get institutionalized, which is when inmates become so used to the prison life that they can't function in the "real world." With such a structured life of being told when to eat, sleep, and use the bathroom, such people get out and are not be able to take care of themselves. These warnings were not in vain. I took every class available. And what I couldn't learn in classes, I went to the library to research.

I learned how to balance a checkbook, though I had never had one. I studied for my driver's license, which I had never had. I researched natural remedies and medical missionary work, anatomy, physiology, nutrition, history, sociology, and mathematics. All of these I knew would play a part somewhere in my life. My entrepreneurial spirit led me to read book after book on business management, economics, and finance. Now to put it all to work!

The Tuesday I was released was the first day of the rest of my life. What would I write on these new pages that God had given me? I took a deep breath of the fresh air. My mom had to return home over an hour away, happy that her boy was going to have a good second start in life. My cabinets were full of good, healthy food. My twin bed was soft and thick, with clean sheets. And I had a TV with 3ABN and eighteen other Adventist channels. I was home.

The next morning, a brother from church picked me up and we headed into town to begin a day of errands. I walked in the DMV and at twenty-nine years old, got my driver's permit. I checked in with my parole officer. Then we went to Goodwill and The Salvation Army, where this brother bought me some good clothes, including a very nice Sabbath suit. I had not been in a suit since my brother and I had walked my mom down the aisle when I was ten years old. But I was glad to have special Sabbath clothes. I was going to visit the King of kings in His house.

Sabbath came before I knew it. I was almost as excited to go to church as I was to get out. For the first time, I would come into the sanctuary of a church, bow on my knees, and give God thanks for His wonderful watch care. I would be able to sit in a Sabbath school class and study the Bible as part of a church family. I would sing and pray, return tithe and give thank offerings, listen to an actual sermon, and be blessed.

As I walked through the doors, I was immediately greeted with a smile and a question. "Welcome! Where are you visiting us from today?" What to say?

"Uhh, well, I grew up in Jefferson City, but I now live in Hallsville, just down the road." I hadn't given much thought to how to respond to all the questions I might get. And they came. I didn't want to scare anyone with my "just out of prison" story. I knew it would come out in time, but I hated the thought of receiving odd stares and questioning looks. At once, I began to wonder who all knew where I had laid my head just a week before.

Moments later, I was introduced to Pastor Larson. He smiled and shook my hand firmly. He already knew about me through the prison ministry team. As soon as I could, I slipped quietly into the sanctuary and sat in the back. Some questions about my acceptance at church remained, but before long I was wrapped up in mission stories, hymns, Sabbath school, and worship. God accepted me, of that I was sure. His people would get to know me in time.

In a couple of days, I had my driver's license and a 2000 Buick LaSabre. It was more than I could have ever asked for. Now, to get a job. My rent was paid for a month and the prison ministries had also paid for my utilities. I needed income. So I went to the career center in Columbia and used their Internet to start looking for job openings and to put in applications. I spent eight to ten hours a day there for most of the next three weeks. No one wanted to hire a felon, especially a dangerous felon.

I polished my résumé and made it look as good as it could with prison jobs for my work history. I mentioned all my studies and certifications. But still the felony was too much. I submitted over 40 applications and résumés to businesses all around town. I got very close to being hired as a computer support specialist, but when it came down to two of us, they chose the other guy. I asked if she could tell me the reason. "It would be just too much of a risk to hire you."

I prayed. I called others to pray. We prayed during prayer meeting. I searched my life to see what could be preventing the Lord's blessing. And I continued to search. I was able to earn $100 painting a porch for one church member, but work was scarce. My sister Amy gave me an old pink laptop computer, for which I was very thankful. I would use my phone's hotspot to connect to the Internet and continue my job hunt.

The constant denials and judgments that I was receiving on an almost daily basis wore heavily on me. I was beginning to get discouraged. I knew God had a plan, but what was it? Now that I was online, I began to network with other Seventh-day Adventists. I found a website called AdventistOnline.com. I was able to meet Adventists from all around the world. It was a social network to discuss theological issues, fulfill prayer requests, and make friends. I needed friends.

My church family was much older than I was. And while they were more than helpful when I needed anything, they were more like parents to me. Where were those my age? I felt lonely. I appreciated the social outlet that these websites afforded. Another website I was recommended to check out by my online friends was TheSingleAdventist.com (TSA). It turned out to be more of a dating and match-making site than a social one, but I set up a profile anyway.

Actually, though I had my two-year plan, I realized that by starting to cultivate a friendship now I might be ready to marry in a couple of years. I figured it would take a year or so to make good, solid friends, maybe more if it was online, then another year for courtship and engagement. Being single was not my long-term calling, of that I was certain. I hungered for companionship, but at the same time I didn't want to rush into anything. I didn't even have a job yet, and I knew that if I was ever to be a provider for a family, I would have to have that down. But that wasn't my biggest hurdle.

I determined that whomever I talked with would need to know about my not-so-nice history. Just an hour or two on TSA proved to me that ladies my age were not looking for an ex-convict with no job. I committed this to the Lord and considered that maybe I was jumping the gun. What did the Lord have planned for me?

A couple of weeks after my release, I received a phone call. It was Elder Neil Dye, the pastor from the Jefferson City and Fulton Missouri churches. "We hear that you have a strong knowledge of the Bible, is that right? Would you like to come down here and go door to door with us? We could use all the help we could get." Absolutely! I would love an opportunity to work for the Master!

So over the next two weeks we knocked on dozens of doors and gave too many surveys to count. We shared literature and struck up interesting conversations. I recall my first door. I watched Pastor Dye and his approach several times. Then it was my turn. All the sudden I was terrified. My mind went blank. I said to myself, "Please don't be home, please don't be home!" But they were. I can't remember exactly what I said, but somehow I got it out. Door to door we went and before long I was really enjoying myself. Now, as I knocked or rang the bell I was saying, "Please *be* home! Please *be* home!"

Between job searching, Internet "socializing," my personal studies, and knocking on doors, I was a very busy man. Then one day when Pastor Dye called, it wasn't about an afternoon of knocking, but rather a career in knocking. He told me that the two churches wanted to hire a Bible worker and that if I was willing, they would hire me. He explained what a Bible worker did and thought that I would do a good job. It wouldn't pay a lot, but it was a lot more than I was making. The church would let me stay in their unfinished basement, so housing would be provided. My mom lived literally four miles from the church, so I could shower at her house. Everything seemed too wonderful to believe. God was truly providing! I told him yes!

Chapter 29
A BUDDING RELATIONSHIP

As a young man in prison, I couldn't help but think about my future and when I would get out. Part of that dreaming included thinking about the type of woman I wanted to marry. I'd had a lot of time to paint in my mind what a "perfect" spouse looked like. I realized that it would take a special someone to accept my past, but I was confident that the right girl was out there. Over the years, I compiled and recompiled a list of character traits that would make up the ideal companion. There were wants and there were needs. Both lists were long, but I was realistic. I knew she would probably have a list too, and I wondered if I had everything on it. Someone once said, "*When I was a young man, I vowed never to marry until I found the ideal woman. Well, I found her—but, alas, she was waiting for the ideal man.*"

I prepared to be a good husband and have a good marriage the best that I knew how. Considering my circumstances, I read every biblically-based marriage and relationship book that I could get my hands on. I saved articles from magazines, did Bible studies, read counsels on relationships, and counseled with older and wiser Christian friends. I wanted to be ready for marriage, should that day come; I could not help but dream of the day I would find my mate.

I had had no real, functional, romantic relationships up to this point, only teenage flings and infatuations. God desired better things for me. Now that I was a Christian, I wanted a relationship that glorified God and was founded on biblical principles. What I discovered was that dating is dangerous, at least as it is normally conducted. Emotions are drawn out and hearts are broken. Infatuation dominates and God is often forgotten. The world's plan of dating often includes "test driving the car before you buy it." I saw studies that directly linked premarital sex to our high divorce rates. "There is a generation that is pure in its own eyes, Yet is not washed from its filthiness" (Proverbs 30:12).

But God's way, once called courtship, falls in line with the biblical principles that lay the foundation for a healthy marriage. Courtship provides a safe place to get to know someone with the clear intention of marriage without hearts being repeatedly drawn out. I knew that God wanted to protect my heart and the heart of the one He was preparing for me. This was the plan I wanted to follow, however odd or unpopular.

"Who can find a virtuous wife? For her worth is far above rubies" (Proverbs 31:10). As I scrolled through the profiles on TSA, I noticed that worldliness had crept into our beloved church. Most of the women were dressed no differently than the way women of the world dressed. I was surprised to see so much jewelry and bare skin. I wondered what kind of men they were trying to attract. But even those who dressed more modestly loved worldly music, junk food, competitive sports, and dancing. I knew I wasn't the model of perfection, but to blatantly flaunt that which we have been counseled against was shocking to me. Weren't we a people getting ready for Jesus to return? Weren't we preparing for the latter rain? As God said,

> I do not pray that You should take them out of the world, but that You should keep them from the evil one. They are not of the world, just as I am not of the world. Sanctify them by Your truth. Your word is truth. (John 17:15–17)

> Do not love the world or the things in the world. If anyone loves the world, the love of the Father is not in him. (1 John 2:15)

Maybe my list was too strict or unrealistic, but I had learned what a godly woman looked like and I knew she existed somewhere. Just as I'd resigned in my mind that finding such a woman might take a while, I came across a profile that was different from the rest. Indeed, I would call it exceptional. Her name was Jenni. She was twenty-seven years old, never married, and with no children. She described herself as compassionate, friendly, and in love with Jesus. She said she was growing daily in Christ, and based on the quality of the books she had said she was currently reading, I could see that this was true. We shared the same hobbies and interests. And to top it all off, she was stunningly beautiful. Everything about her shined with Jesus' character. After taking it all in, I sat back in my chair and talked with God.

"Lord, you know that I want to get married someday. I am finding it hard to discover a woman who loves you more than anything. But now it seems I may have found her. Father, if it be Your will, I want to marry this girl."

That day, within minutes of reading about her and seeing her picture, I knew that this girl was the one I wanted to marry! I asked Him to give me the desire of my heart. From a human perspective, I suppose this might appear presumptuous, but from God's angle, I can understand it now. He had a plan.

This was exactly one week before I was offered the Bible worker position by Pastor Dye. As I was without work, I wasn't sure what she would say. TSA allowed us to instant message those we would like to talk to or leave a message on their "wall." The few ladies I had chatted with so far had invariably asked what kind of work I did. But all things considered, I still felt the go-ahead from God, so I sent her a message while measuring every word: "Hi Jenni. From what I read on your profile, I see you are a serious-minded Adventist, not caught up with the world. This is quite rare. I would love to hear back from you if you are interested in a like-minded friend."

I waited for a few days with no return message. I was a little discouraged as I didn't know what was going on her end. I would check periodically to see if she responded, but I found absolutely nothing. I knew there were no other girls like her anywhere! On Friday, July 27, the day after I was hired as a Bible worker, I saw that she was online at that time and I again asked the Lord if I should pursue her. And, praise the Lord, with His permission, I sent her an instant message.

Almost immediately she responded with a cheerful greeting!

Jenni:

As I responded to the instant message that Wyatt sent me, I faintly recalled seeing his profile picture in my inbox saying he had sent me a note. But I couldn't find the note anywhere. But now, with his instant message, I saw his picture again. Before responding, I hit the link to his profile and, after I read it, wondered to myself how I had overlooked this wonderful guy. As we chatted, my positive impression from his profile was confirmed in a sweet exchange as we got to know each other.

But when, in the first five minutes of the conversation, he opened up to me about his past, I was in for a surprise. Our conversation went something like this:

Jenni: So, what do you do for a living?

Wyatt: I start a new Bible worker job next week.

Jenni: Great! What did you do before Bible work?

Wyatt: Well, It's complicated.

At this point, I was thinking, "How complicated can it be? He must not have worked at all." I sadly jumped to the possible conclusion that he was lazy or was living off of his mother until this job.

As quickly as the thought crossed my mind, Wyatt typed on:

Wyatt: Actually, I have something I think you deserve to know right from the start...

Jenni: Ok...

I could feel that the conversation had taken a serious tone. I waited for what he needed to tell me. What he shared next surprised me, and yet was not as shocking to me as someone might think.

Wyatt: I just got out of prison on June 19. I went to prison when I was 15 and served 14 years.

I thought, "Wow! What he did must have been bad." I wondered what he had done. As I quickly considered if it was appropriate to ask what he was sentenced for, Wyatt answered my un-typed question.

Wyatt: I was sentenced for assault with a deadly weapon.

As I considered this brief exchange, we continued the conversation:

Wyatt: I totally understand if you don't want to talk to me...

Jenni: No, I want to talk. Surprisingly it doesn't bother me. Do you mind if I ask some questions?

Wyatt: Sure. Go ahead.

We continued to chat and get to know each other. Wyatt's honesty and openness drew me to want to know him more. I knew sharing something like this was hard to do, especially in the first five minutes of a conversation. It showed me that he had a sincere desire to protect my heart.

Two years earlier, I would never have considered being friends with someone who had gone to prison. Unfortunately, I didn't have too much compassion for law breakers. Like many who do not have close loved ones who committed a crime and went to prison, I had come to view all inmates as bad. I didn't write them off as unreachable, but prison ministry was never something I considered very successful.

My outlook changed in the spring of 2010. I was in a relationship with a nice guy. Our relationship ended when I realized we were not a match. Several months after we broke up, I found out that he went to prison for crimes he had committed before I met him. I went through many emotions as I registered the reality that my friend was worthy of prison time and that he would serve time for the next ten years! I chose to keep in touch with him while he was in prison and tried to be a friend and encourage him. The whole experience changed my thoughts toward convicts. It was a paradigm shift in my life. I realized that not all those in prison are bad people. They are people who need help, people who have made bad decisions, and are paying the consequences. And in fact, some are repentant and desire to change their lives. This experience paved the way to open my heart and mind to being willing to talk with Wyatt.

We expanded our chats to email and would exchange very lengthy and detailed messages. I could not wait for the next email to come. Sometimes we would exchange more than one a day! I recognized quickly that he was a converted man, one that I was compatible with, and one that I could see myself marrying. After several days of emailing we started to instant message on Skype.

Wyatt:

I had never been in love before. Was that what this was? What I found was that each email we exchanged touched my heart deeper and deeper and was confirming more and more that we were right for each other. Yes, love was growing, though we didn't dare admit it quite yet. We asked each other every conceivable question. I began this journey just looking for a "friend" who, in time, would prove to be my match.

What I didn't expect was just how fast it would move. It was clear that I had eyes only for Jenni, and so I began to pursue her.

Jenni:

I spent a lot of time in prayer about Wyatt as I was getting to know him. I soon found that there were no guys online I had met that I wanted to continue talking with except Wyatt. He eventually worked up the nerve to ask for my phone number, and that evening he called me. Our first phone conversation lasted seven hours and the next day, August 15th, my journal entry was titled "He's the one!" I wrote: *All I can say is that I really like this man, and he is amazing, I really feel like he is the one for me. ... I think Wyatt is my match.*

I also called several friends that day as well as my mom and expressed my utter joy in getting to know Wyatt. I had never believed that one could know so soon, but I shared how I was pretty sure that "Wyatt is my husband."

Chapter 30
OUR COURTSHIP

Wyatt:

My relationship with Jenni had been unconventional from the beginning. Her parents lived in Hawaii, but I wanted their blessing before moving from the "special friend" stage to the next level. Ruling out an expensive plane ride to ask them in person I settled on sending her mom a message through Facebook, the only way I knew how. On August 21, 2012, I wrote:

> *My name is Wyatt Allen. Jenni says that she has talked to you about me. Believe me, I talk to my mom about Jenni all the time. As you know, we are both beginning to like each other very much and while I am scared to death about not knowing what to do, I do know that I wanted to ask you and your husband's permission before I moved very far. As Adventists we believe in courting, as you know, and while I don't know everything about how everything is supposed to work, I do believe this is a time where two people are considering the possibility of marriage down the road and getting to know each other better to see if they would be a good match. It is more than just dating, but also far from an engagement. I would be honored if I could have the blessing of you and your husband in moving forward with this relationship. I can't tell you how excited I am to have met someone so wonderful as your daughter. She is a precious jewel! I would especially value the approval of Jenni's father. Thank you for your time, Mrs. Lane. And may God bless you abundantly!*
>
> Sincerely, Wyatt Allen

I waited as patiently as I could for the reply. It came the next day. Wilma, her mother, told me that they had great faith in Jenni's judgment and if she approved, then they did as well. She recognized it was still early in the relationship but they were encouraged that I was a "devout Adventist Christian."

I was elated. She knew about my past too and still she approved! I wrote her again:

> *Thank you so much for your favorable response. I too look forward to speaking with you. I can't tell you how nervous and excited I am that I have been drawing closer to Jenni. She sure is a special girl, and I know that no guy will ever be fully worthy of her, but should this lead in that direction, I assure you that I will care for her and love with every fiber of my being and make you, her parents, proud of her selection. It is true that we are in the "early days" of our relationship, but as we grow closer to the Lord and to each other, I hope to also get to know you better. Pray for us not to move too quickly or too slowly, but right at the pace the Lord wants us to.*
>
> *Blessings always, Wyatt.*

While I had the permission to move to the next level, I had to be sure she was on the same page. We now talked daily on the phone and face to face through Skype. Our emails were getting longer and more specific. So I continued to pursue. I was aware she had a "list" like I had (though we didn't share the contents with one another). Did I match up? Needs and wants. Apparently there were a lot of them on her list as there was on mine. She fit just about everything that I desired in a wife. I was praying much more about this than about anything else. I considered this inspired counsel:

> If men and women are in the habit of praying twice a day before they contemplate marriage, they should pray four times a day when such a step is anticipated. Marriage is something that will influence and affect your life, both in this world and in the world to come. (*The Adventist Home*, 71)

Jenni:

As we continued to talk about everything under the sun, our hearts were becoming knit together. Wyatt was actively pursuing and that was obvious. Getting little impromptu poems in my email right before bed and hearing sweet unexpected compliments were common. But it was more than the wooing that drew me to Wyatt. I saw in him a beautiful picture of Jesus Christ and a man that I could respect and love. As I continued to get to know Wyatt more checkmarks were being added to "my man" list. He certainly was matching up! I had often wondered if my hopes of the qualities I desired in a man were too idealistic, and perhaps some parts were, but I was seeing God give me the desires of my heart!

We knew things were "going fast" in the typical way of looking at time. We often talked about the timing of things; our views on how timing of relationship, courtship, and marriage should go. Since both of us had not had a biblically-based adult relationship up to this point in our lives, we shared what we had learned from our Bible studies and reading on the subject. We did our best to base our relationship on this knowledge. We considered our ages, our stations in life, and our financial status. We didn't want emotions or feelings to get in the way of hearing God's voice on the matter.

Wyatt:

Yes, it was fast, but never rushed. It was a natural progression that brought me to the date of September 7, 2012. I was ready to ask her. I had permission from God and from her parents. Now the question was, would she consent?

Jenni:

On the morning of September 7, Wyatt told me that he had a poem that he had written for me. He had already composed several of them in my honor, which I loved! I actually write poetry myself and have a high appreciation for it. We were on Skype video and I was able to see his expressions as he read the following poem to me:

Just the Beginning

How do I put thoughts into speech?
How do I give voice to the heart?
How do I stretch beyond my reach,
And the best words impart?

With the help of God our King
And His angels there besides,
I will to you the truth bring
As in His way, me He guides.

I've realized for a while now
As I've examined my heart's desire,
As on my knees I did bow
Often at God's throne to inquire,

That my heart is yours, my love,
For not another one to share,
You alone stand clear above
Any other one beyond compare.

Love indeed is the motive within,
Heaven-born love for you;
I know it now; I've known it then,
But it is time now that you knew…

Just how fond of you I've become,
How desperately in love I've grown,
How ready I am to honorably come,
To you and make my love known.

So, Jenni, I ask with trembling indeed,
Knowing exactly where it does lead
To move with me, yes to proceed
To courtship where we can succeed,

At being a couple who lives unto the King;
A pair who seeks Him first in all;
And closer to Him each other to bring,
To lead one another to heed His call.

To be bound to Him with all our heart,
And then to each other we can start
To grow into a love that is not just in part,
But one from which we shall never depart.

Courtship is a time to see if we are one,
Growing in a relationship with which God can agree.
And so let me ask you, if your heart I've won,
Will you consider spending the rest of your life with me?

I gladly said yes! And so our courtship began. We decided to continue to get to know each other with the intention of marriage in view.

Wyatt:

She said "Yes!" The wonder of it is that we had come so far so fast and we had not yet met each other face to face. This concerned some of her friends who loved and cared for her, but we could both see God leading. Courtship was not final. We were both aware that God could still lead us in two different directions. We were prepared for that, but all the evidences and providences were pressing us together. Our next plan was to meet in person!

And this is how God worked that out: I was invited to speak at a family camp meeting in the beginning of October, just a few hours from where I lived. Jenni had actually attended this family camp meeting before and knew several people who regularly came. We decided that this would be a perfect place to have the opportunity to spend some time getting to know each other better and to be around people we both knew. It appeared that our personalities, our likes and dislikes, and our views on almost every topic agreed perfectly. But there was still a need to spend much time with the other person and to observe how they interacted with others.

With Jenni's job as a 24-hour baby nurse, she would be committed for weeks at a time to working with a family of a newborn. Knowing her tight schedule, I still ventured to invite her to family camp meeting. A few days later we learned that it was not only possible for her to come, but it was almost as if the Lord had orchestrated it Himself. We were getting ready to meet in about a month's time!

I was to meet her at the airport in St. Louis on October 4, and drive her directly to Camp Heritage at the Lake of the Ozarks. Phone calls, emails, and even face-to-face video chats did not prepare me for the exciting day when I would actually see her coming down the terminal. I was terrified and thrilled at the same time. I was meeting, in person, for the first time, the woman that I would possibly marry. There she was. I was struck by her beauty and melted by her countenance. Could all this be real!?! It was really her.

Jenni:

I was so excited to be meeting Wyatt in person. I already felt like I had known him for years. I called Wyatt as I made my way to baggage claim. I thought Wyatt was going to park in the cellphone lot and that when I called him, he would drive around to pick me up with my bags. On the phone I asked him where he was, then he turned it around and asked me where I was without answering the question. Little did I know, he was waiting near baggage claim. He wanted to surprise me. I turned the corner as I explained where I was and there *he* was at the end of the walk! We hung up the phone and quickly walked toward each other and gave each other a hug. Then Wyatt put a real flower lei around my neck. I was so impressed that he had brought the Hawaiian tradition to St. Louis. I felt very special. I'm sure it was the first flower lei ever given in the St. Louis airport.

We made our way to the car, chatting along the way. We both had a permanent smile attached to our faces. I felt completely at ease in Wyatt's presence and all my nervousness melted away. I felt like I was with an old friend. Our long ride there went by fast as we talked about life—our life.

Wyatt:

Three hours later, we arrived at the camp grounds ready for the excitement of the meetings. But dare I say, I was more excited about who walked with me and who looked at me with such kindness and love. Everything I had hoped for was confirmed in this woman named Jenni. I got to see so many sides to her and all of them shone with the character of Jesus. Jenni had worked it out with my pastor and his wife that after camp meeting was over she would stay with them for about 10 more days! During the two weeks we got to spend together we were inseparable. She fixed meals for us, came with me and sat in on the many Bible studies I gave, and joined me for family worship. But time flew by so fast!

Jenni eventually had to fly back to Georgia. The trip back to the airport wasn't as happy as the one from there, but it was filled with hope. We talked about the next time we would meet and the progression of our relationship. And then she was off. When would we see each other again? God had that worked out too!

Jenni:

I watched Wyatt over our time together at the camp meeting and while he did his work as a Bible worker. I wanted to get to know his character in person. On the second day at camp, we were waiting in line at the cafeteria and I noticed that the stack of trays was getting low. I wondered if the kitchen staff knew about it and was glancing around the room for trays. Then as I turned back around, there was Wyatt restacking them. Wow. Did he read my mind? I was really impressed that he had noticed the problem as quickly as I did and was even more impressed that he did something about it without being asked.

In my bunkhouse were a mother and her two children. The boy, whose name was Truth, was about nine years old. When it got colder than expected, Wyatt volunteered to loan Truth his stocking cap for the walk before the evening meeting. I thought that was gentlemanly of him. He returned it before going to bed. But on the way to breakfast the next morning, Truth wondered out loud if Wyatt might bring the cap again because it was even colder that day. When he saw him and began to ask him about it, he didn't even have the words completely out of his mouth before Wyatt pulled the warm stocking cap from his back pocket and handed it to him. If the boy wasn't amazed, I certainly was! I liked him more and more. But as impressed as I was, I was still cautious to guard my heart and Wyatt's too.

When I got home to my little town in Georgia, a friend in whom I had confided asked me, "So, was he everything you thought he would be, now that you have met in person?" I answered, "He is more than I could have ever hoped for! He is amazing!" Amazing became my favorite adjective to describe Wyatt Edward Allen.

Chapter 31
AN ENGAGING WOMAN

Jenni's Version:

On New Year's Eve 2012, I did not realize a new phase of my life would begin!

I spent the day with my mom and my sister Crystal, who were visiting. They were there to meet Wyatt, who also came to visit, and to chaperone our time together. We did not really plan anything special for bringing in the New Year, but Wyatt did suggest that we both write out our New Year's resolutions so we could read them to each other at midnight. It had been years since I'd brought in the New Year awake. I told him that I wasn't interested in staying up since I stay up with newborns most of the year for my job. But since it was Wyatt's last day in town and my family wanted to stay up as well, I conceded.

As the evening wore on, we had dinner and played a board game together. We tried to figure out how to bring in the New Year and how I would spend my remaining time with Wyatt before he went back to Missouri. He kept asking me if there was any special place in Trion or a lookout or something fun to do in town. "Trion, Georgia?" I thought. "Not a chance in this little town. Besides, my favorite place is pretty much at church or home." Little did I know, I was not helping very much. He was trying to find a good place to propose to me at the dawning of the New Year!

We finally decided to go to a nearby town about forty minutes away to spend some time together bowling. Neither Mom nor Crystal knew, at this point, that Wyatt was going to propose. He was concerned that their excitement would ruin the surprise.

Right before we left, while I was in my room getting ready, Wyatt told my mom and sister about his plans to ask for my hand in marriage at midnight. He also solicited their help in the surprise.

When I came out completely clueless but ready to go bowling, I asked, "Are you guys sure you don't want to come with us?"

Mom and Crystal played it off well, "No, honey. You go ahead and have fun. We are just going to hang out here. We will see you around midnight to bring in the New Year."

So Wyatt and I left to go bowling.

Mom and Crystal went to Wal-Mart and purchased flowers and extension cords—his plan was coming together.

We had a great time together, though we decided that bowling was not for us. I had no idea what was up Wyatt's sleeve. When we got to the corner near my home, Wyatt told me to close my eyes because he had a surprise for me. I was intrigued and the thought flashed into my mind of a possible proposal but I quickly dismissed the thought. I knew we were going to exchange resolutions that night, so figured his "surprise" was something romantic for that occasion.

After we pulled into the driveway, my eyes still closed, Wyatt led me by the hand to the gazebo and had me open my eyes. There was beautiful quiet music playing and the gazebo was decorated with white lights and flowers. It was very romantic! But I still did not suspect anything because Wyatt is always romantic! It was just a little before midnight and it was time for us to read our New Year's resolutions to each other. They were the perfect cover-up for why there was such a romantic atmosphere at the gazebo. I had no idea. I thought he just wanted a nice first New Year's Eve together.

We went back and forth sharing our resolutions for the new year as we heard fireworks in the distance. After we finished, Wyatt said he had written a poem for me. This was not uncommon for Wyatt either. He loves to write poetry for me, and I love to hear it. He is so talented! As he read me the poem, I still didn't realize what he was doing until about half way through. Then I started to get suspicious. The last two stanzas of the poem made it clear! He finished the poem, got down on one knee and held my hands and asked me to marry him.

I said YES.

Here is the lovely engagement poem he wrote for me on that unforgettable night:

Another Year Dawns

By Wyatt Allen
December 31, 2012

On the cusp of another year I reflect on the past.
Mistakes many and time gone fast.
Redeeming the time is now my main concern;
Turning from self and sin and from my past to learn.

Jesus is coming, oh, coming so very soon.
With Him daily, nay, hourly, I commit to commune,
As I seek His will for the time that now remains,
Until He returns and in His kingdom then reigns.

The year before us now promises to be
One of adventure of the highest degree.
As we keep our eyes fixed on Him from above
And grow for each other in His type of love.

Jenni Rose, my love, how I've grown to adore
Your heart of kindness and your character so pure.
I've been delighted with you as my heart has been tied,
With yours in Christ all together unified.

Thankfulness ascends while on my past I reflect,
On how the Lord Has led and His providences connect.
Freedom was granted at the moment just right,
That led from that time to be right here tonight.

From the day that we met and began to believe
That our lives may have been meant to interweave.
Step by step learning, growing, and knowing
'Till our hearts were entwined with every love bestowing.

Examining closely our values, our interests, our desires,
Our characters, our plans, and to what each other aspires,
We longed to see if the Lord is leading us to be
Together as Wyatt Edward and Jenni Rose Marie.

We have closely listened to the Shepherd's voice
As He leads us to understand our best choice.
His Providence, His soft heart whisper, His Holy Word;
Each has spoken clearly and this is what I've heard:

That Jenni, you are the one that God has designed for me;
To love and protect to be all you need me to be.
That God has orchestrated us to be together forever;
To be one with each other and never to sever.

I know without a doubt that there is not one as fit,
To be my companion on earth and to forever commit.
So I ask you now, with love from deep within:
Would you consent to be Jenni Rose Marie Allen?

Wyatt's version:

It may sound a bit unromantic to tell how it all worked out from my perspective, but there is more to the story.

On Sunday, December 9, I officially asked Mr. Lane for the honor of having his daughter's hand in marriage. He thankfully said yes. I told him that I wasn't sure exactly when I was going to ask, but that I was sure I was going to at some point in the near future. I knew she was the one for me! We talked for almost two hours that day discussing the future and some ideas for a perfect proposal.

I thought long and hard about the best way to ask her. I only had a few absolutes to work with: I had to surprise her, it had to be creative, and I had to be sure she would say yes. I was 99.99% sure she would. God had clearly been leading us together and we both could see it. But the how, when, and where were still up in the air.

I finally hit on it! I would do a scavenger hunt. I was sure she had never heard of that idea. So I started working on it. I knew I would be visiting her from December 20 until January 1, so I decided that when the time was just right I would do it. Then I began to plan.

I started writing poems to be placed at strategic spots all around Trion and Summerville, spots that at one point had a significant meaning for the two of us. The plan was that she would awake and find a note which said:

Good morning my love, whom I greatly adore;
    Today has an adventure for you in store.
Get yourself ready, if you need, take your time.
    You're off for a trip that will be sublime!

I present you with a clue, one that you know
    When you are ready off you will go.
Think of the place where once you had need,
    To fix all four feet of your electronic steed.

Talk to the keeper of the shop of candy name fame;
    He shall have the next clue in this exciting little game.
Follow it from there; to another clue it shall lead.
    Be careful on the road, Jenni, don't dare speed.

This would take her to Reese's Tire Service where we got new tires for her SUV. The mechanic there would then give her the next clue:

Head next to the place where oft' you sent
    Emails of love, thoughts, and good intent;
Where quiet you must be to even talk to me,
    Or trouble you'll receive and out you'll be.

On a bench you would sit and chat with me
    Asking lots of questions, my character to see.
Now go inside and search till you find
    The next clue for you as this game we unwind.

Searching for the name whose title is true,
    It expresses the truth of the heart that belongs to you,
By Noris Kern even a child can see
    There you will find the clue for thee.

The Public Library had a children's book named *I'll Love You Forever* which held the next clue. Eventually she would end up at her church at Summerville, with me waiting at the altar on my knee. That *was* the plan! Romantic right?

Well—here's what happened. I was planning to go to Georgia on the 20th and drive the ten hours or so to her house. What I didn't expect was that on December 13 she would be at my mom's house waiting on *me*. She flew one way to see me as a late birthday present and so we could drive back together to Georgia the next week. So I got to spend a whole extra week with her! And what a week it was, too! We visited more of my Bible students, we went to the zoo, and we went to church together.

On our long drive to her house, the topic of marriage proposals came up (was she on to me?). She told me a tragic story of one man who did a scavenger hunt (of all things!) that went terribly wrong. He left her in the rain and waiting at McDonald's and it just got worse from there. *Gulp!* She knew about the scavenger hunt idea after all. And it didn't sound like she liked the idea—at least not if she got stuck waiting in the rain. But that's not all.

Then, as we were visiting with her best friend, Tara, and her husband Esteban over Christmas, I got the private opportunity to ask them about how he had proposed to her. They told me the whole story. It was so romantic. The problem was that it was almost *exactly* like my plan! Even with the scavenger hunt ending at the church altar! I knew Jenni knew the story too, so what was I to do?

Time was running out and I had to scrap the whole plan and just start over. I began to pray and think. Think and pray. It was December 31. I was leaving the next day to go back to Missouri. It started off like any normal day, but after family worship and breakfast, I excused myself to my room and began to work in earnest on my plan.

I knew what I would do. I would propose to her at midnight after exchanging New Year's resolutions. It was a perfect plan. So I knew the when and the how. But now I needed to know the where. I began asking for romantic spots in town that held a special place for her. Nothing. She said church and home. That was it. Then I suggested the resolution idea at midnight, but I quickly found out that she was not a fan of staying up late. She said that it had been years since she had stayed up that late on New Year's Eve. (Not to mention that we'd had some interesting conversations about temperance and proper sleep habits.) But alas, she finally consented.

But where? At this point, I was desperate. I not only had to make it a surprise, it also had to be romantic. Her living room would not cut it. To complicate matters, she was insisting that her mom and sister go with us to do something. My intentions were hidden to them as well. I was confident that my plan would sufficiently throw her off the trail, but all day I was casually asking what she wanted to do, as if there was no plan that I was orchestrating. I kept asking her where she wanted to exchange our New Year's resolutions.

I spent more time in my room composing the poem she shared above. It had to be just perfect. We had fun playing a board game and getting to know her family more. But still I wondered where! I took a step outside at about 5:00 PM to catch some fresh air and to think—and that is when I saw it—her gazebo. She had shared with me long before about her dream to restore it to its original beauty. There was no time for that, but it was a perfect spot to do what I had been dreaming of doing for a while now. But I needed help; it was time to recruit.

I caught Crystal first while Jenni was back in her room. I asked her, "Can you keep a secret?" She smiled mischievously, expecting some juicy inside info.

"Yes, of course!" she said.

I told her that I was going to ask her sister to marry me *that night* and that I needed her help in making it happen. I laid out the plan:

I would take Jenni bowling and would finish up just in time to come back minutes before midnight. I wanted to have the gazebo decorated with white Christmas lights and flowers, and to have quiet mellow music playing in the background. I put cash in her hand with a shopping list and asked her if she could help. Her eyes were wide and excited. I was hoping that her excitement wouldn't tip Jenni off. She went and told her mom about my plan and we were able to meet for a minute more to go over some last little details.

Then we left. On the way we drove by the Summerville town gazebo all lit up with dazzling white lights. Jenni saw it and commented on how beautiful it was. If I had only known! To throw her off, I told her that when we came back we could stop by if we had time and if no one was there (of course I expected people to be there at midnight and for us not to have time). We went bowling, which I had not done since I was about fourteen years old. The loud, unchristian music drove us out early, but with a couple of detours we were right on schedule to get home at midnight.

As we got near, I had her close her eyes and prepare for a surprise. I was hoping she would chalk it up to romance and not suspect that I was going to propose, but I had no other option. We got out, and as I led her to the gazebo, I pressed play on what turned out to be her favorite CD (thanks, Crystal!). By her smile I could see that she was happy. We pulled out our typed-up resolutions. Then right before we began to read, she paused and asked if she could go in to use the restroom real quick—she had to go. Oh, no! If she went inside, her mom and sister would be in there shouting "Congratulations!" I couldn't let that happen so I asked her to hold it. I told her we wouldn't be long. Cruel? Maybe, but it was worth it! We alternated through our many New Year's resolutions while shivering in the midnight cold. It was just past that time when I pulled out my poem that I had composed just hours before. Here goes, I told myself.

I read the poem while looking into her eyes as much as I could. Dropping to one knee, I looked up into her radiant face and posed the question I had longed to ask since I asked God's permission to make her my wife. She said yes. She said YES! We embraced for what seemed forever, looked at each other longingly, and then we shared a kiss that I will always remember. Abruptly she pushed me back by my shoulders and said, "Wait! Did you ask my dad?" I assured her that I had. She smiled widely and held me again.

We prayed together and went into the house where Jenni's mom and sister were anxiously awaiting us with shouts of congratulations. I thanked them profusely for a job well done. It couldn't have been better. Jenni was genuinely surprised. She thought it was creative. And she said yes. Thus began the year 2013.

Chapter 32
GOD MEANT IT FOR GOOD

In a world where so many people are asking, "Why me, Lord?" or "Why does God allow bad things to happen to good people?" I stand as a testimony of God's goodness and His love. My life, littered with sin and evil, plagued with a past of shame and selfishness, proves that there exists a sin-hating, sinner-loving Creator. When I was heading for a bridge down the road, God stepped in and saved me from certain destruction.

I am not the first to say that prison was my salvation. Even my father, when he was alive, would tell me that I would probably have been dead had it not been for my incarceration. Why did God count me worthy of His grace? Why did He not give up on me when any reasonable person would have? It was because of His love. The Bible says, "God is love" (1 John 4:8, 16). In that love, He wants a relationship with me. He wants to live with me forever. He sent His son as a sacrifice to make that possible.

> Who is a God like You, pardoning iniquity and passing over the transgression of the remnant of His heritage? He does not retain His anger forever, because He delights in mercy. He will again have compassion on us, and will subdue our iniquities. You will cast all our sins into the depths of the sea. (Micah 7:18, 19)

It was God's love that won me. It is God's love that keeps me. It is God's love that compels me to share my story of redemption.

Though Joseph would "do time" in a prison, I saw myself more in the lives of his brothers than in his life. They conceived murder in their hearts. The Bible says, "Now when they saw him afar off, even before he came near them, they conspired against him to kill him" (Genesis 37:18). In the end, they sold Joseph into slavery without one care for his future.

While he spent the next thirteen years in both slavery and prison, it was the brothers who lived in bondage. "Do you not know that to whom you present yourselves slaves to obey, you are that one's slaves whom you obey, whether of sin leading to death, or of obedience leading to righteousness?" (Romans 6:16). They lived with the double guilt of selling their brother and of lying to their father about him. "And all his sons and all his daughters arose to comfort him; but he refused to be comforted, and he said, 'For I shall go down into the grave to my son in mourning.' Thus his father wept for him" (Genesis 37:35). Every time they saw their father, they were reminded of their crime and could find no peace.

Joseph rose from the degradation of his chains through the mighty providence of God to become vice-pharaoh over all Egypt. In this position, he was able to provide food for all the land, including the land of his birth. When, in the course of time, "Joseph made himself known to his brothers" they were in absolute shock (See Genesis 45:1, 3). What would he do to them? What vengeance would now be his?

But Joseph said to them, "Do not therefore be grieved or angry with yourselves because you sold me here; for God sent me before you to preserve life. … And God sent me before you to preserve a posterity for you in the earth, and to save your lives by a great deliverance. So now it was not you who sent me here, but God; and He has made me a father to Pharaoh, and lord of all his house, and a ruler throughout all the land of Egypt" (Genesis 45:5, 7, 8).

Joseph went to great lengths to demonstrate his love and forgiveness. Three times he declared that it was God who sent him to Egypt, not the brothers. He had a heart to save them, not destroy them. But even seventeen years later, they proved that they still did not know their brother, thinking that his honor for their father kept Joseph's wrath at bay:

> When Joseph's brothers saw that their father was dead, they said, "Perhaps Joseph will hate us, and may actually repay us for all the evil which we did to him." So they sent messengers to Joseph, saying, "…Now, please, forgive the trespass of the servants of the God of your father." And Joseph wept when they spoke to him.

Then his brothers also went and fell down before his face, and they said, "Behold, we are your servants."

Joseph said to them, "Do not be afraid, for am I in the place of God? But as for you, you meant evil against me; but God meant it for good, in order to bring it about as it is this day, to save many people alive. Now therefore, do not be afraid; I will provide for you and your little ones." And he comforted them and spoke kindly to them. (Genesis 50:15–21)

Finally, they learned that his mercy was authentic. His motivation was love. I can see their hearts melt by such an expression and the respect and honor they had from him from that day forth. He had every reason to destroy them, but he didn't.

God is calling us to see Him as He really is. Satan has distorted the picture of the Almighty, painting Him as arbitrary and cruel. We are taught that He is distant "though He is not far from each one of us" (Acts 17:27). We are taught that a hell without end is compatible with His character of love and justice. We are taught that He doesn't care how we live, or what we eat, or who we marry, even though the Bible teaches that God cares very much about our happiness in every area of our lives. When we believe these lies, when we buy into the falsehoods about God, we will be negatively affected. Some will be lost for serving out of fear and not love. Some will be lost for rejecting God because they didn't understand Him. Some will be lost forever because they simply couldn't believe that God really loved them and desired to save them.

God sent me to prison. He had a purpose in it. It was to save me alive to this day. It was to teach me the character lessons needed in the great controversy that wages between Christ and Satan. It was to give me the opportunity to learn what God really looks like. It was to give me an opportunity to show myself approved, a workman who needs not to be ashamed. He loved me and He sent me to prison so I could be set free.

Chapter 33
THE LEAST OF THE LEAST

Who is the least of the least? Notice what Jesus said:

> Then the King will say to those on His right hand, "Come, you blessed of My Father, inherit the kingdom prepared for you from the foundation of the world: for I was hungry and you gave Me food; I was thirsty and you gave Me drink; I was a stranger and you took Me in; I was naked and you clothed Me; I was sick and you visited Me; I was in prison and you came to Me."
>
> Then the righteous will answer Him, saying, "Lord, when did we see You hungry and feed You, or thirsty and give You drink? When did we see You a stranger and take You in, or naked and clothe You? Or when did we see You sick, or in prison, and come to You?" And the King will answer and say to them, "Assuredly, I say to you, inasmuch as you did it to one of the least of these My brethren, you did it to Me." (Matthew 25:34–40)

In His list of the leasts, Jesus lists those in prison last. By His own definition the prisoners are not just the least, but they are the "least of the least." Though all may forget the plight of these precious souls, God does not. He identifies with them. He feels for them and seeks to comfort them. Jesus loves the least. Paul writes, "Whereof I was made a minister, according to the gift of the grace of God given unto me by the effectual working of his power. Unto me, who am less than the least of all saints, is this grace given, that I should preach among the Gentiles the unsearchable riches of Christ." And again, "But God has chosen the foolish things of the world to put to shame the wise, and God has chosen the weak things of the world to put to shame the things which are mighty; and the base things of the world and the things which are despised God has chosen, and the things which are not, to bring to nothing the things that are, that no flesh should glory in His presence." (Ephesians 3:7, 8 KJV; 1 Corinthians 1:27–29)

A few go to prison because they were falsely accused. Some are there for political reasons. Others are persecuted for their faith, as were Peter, Paul, and Silas. But the grand majority of those incarcerated in prisons around the world are those who have committed grievous crimes. The Scriptures make no distinction when we are admonished to "remember them that are in bonds, as bound with them" (Hebrews 13:3 KJV). Psalm 69:33 says, "For the Lord hears the poor, and does not despise His prisoners." Neither should we.

I recall those who in the Scriptures at one time spent time in custody: Joseph, Samson, Jeremiah, Micaiah, Zedekiah, Manasseh, Daniel, John the Baptist, Peter, James, John, Silas, Paul, Epaphras, Andronicus, Junia, and even Jesus Himself were arrested. I think of Samson and Manasseh especially, who during their time in captivity sought the Lord and repented. Samson is mentioned in the faith chapter (Hebrews 11) and Manasseh went back to reigning as king over Judah (See Hebrews 11:32; 2 Chronicles 33:11–16). I could repeat with them the precious words of Scripture, "It is good for me that I have been afflicted, that I may learn Your statutes" (Psalm 119:71).

For over fourteen years, I was the least of the least. During that time, there were men and women who volunteered their time to minister to me and to others. They saw Jesus in prison grays, dressed in stripes, and in orange jumpsuits. They felt it their duty and privilege to speak words of hope and show by their actions that they cared. While certainly not all are called to reach out to those in juvenile halls, jails, prisons, and treatment centers, those that do are making a difference for eternity. Jesus said, "I have not come to call the righteous, but sinners, to repentance" (Luke 5:32).

They wrote letters that would come at just the right time. I read and reread the letters that I received. A personal letter is worth its weight in gold when in prison; it shows that someone cares. The encouragement and counsel those letters contained helped to see me through many hardships. Because there are so many prisoners who have scammed kind and sacrificing church members, I found that there are very few willing to write. "As cold waters to a thirsty soul, so is good news from a far country" (Proverbs 25:25).

Visits were the most personal of all. During my time inside I received visits from pastors, elders, and elderly ladies. Friends who got to know me over the years would often come and see me as well. When I received honor status by staying conduct-violation free, I was allowed to have a food visit where the visitors could bring in a home-cooked meal. How precious were those visits! Of them it will be said by Jesus, "I was in prison and you visited me."

Paul had a vision almost two thousand years ago in which a man of Macedonia asked him, "Come over to Macedonia and help us." Luke reports that, "after he had seen the vision, immediately we sought to go to Macedonia, concluding that the Lord had called us to preach the gospel to them" (Acts 16:9, 10). Paul obeyed the divine call and notice the results: Lydia and her household were saved and later the Philippian church was raised up. Interestingly, it was here in Philippi, because of his obedience, that Paul ended up "doing time" himself. They held a worship service with praying and singing hymns—at midnight! Not only did the prisoners listen to these "ambassadors in bonds," but that very night even a jailer and his family gave their hearts to Jesus.

Do those in prison have any less need to hear the everlasting gospel preached to them than did the Macedonians? Could it be said about prison ministry: "The harvest truly is great, but the laborers are few; therefore pray the Lord of the harvest to send out laborers into His harvest" (Luke 10:2)? May it be remembered that, "None are so vile, none have fallen so low, as to be beyond the working of this power. In all who will submit themselves to the Holy Spirit a new principle of life is to be implanted; the lost image of God is to be restored in humanity" (*Christ's Object Lessons*, 96).

May the blessings of Almighty God be upon those who have sacrificed their time, their energies, their money, and sometimes even their reputation to minister to inmates. Whether it is through preaching, teaching, singing, playing instruments, or simply just being there, their reward shall not be forgotten. God generously rewards those who sacrifice for those who cannot repay (Matthew 6:3; Luke 14:14; Proverbs 19:17). Interestingly, I have heard several "outmates" say that they are tremendously blessed by their coming week after week.

It is important to consider that upwards of 95% of all of those in prison will one day be out of prison. They will stand behind you at the checkout counter, sit in front of you at church, or walk next to you down the street. They may very well be your neighbor next door.

Would you rather they be a Spirit-filled, Christ-following, Bible-believing Christian, or just the same person they were when they first went into the penitentiary? We can make a difference now and for eternity by sowing seeds of redemption and hope among those who desperately need it.

Chapter 34

PRINCIPALITIES AND POWERS

The moment one takes a stand for Jesus and truth is the same moment the enemy of souls commits to wage full blown war against them. We see the fruits of the demonic possession and oppression today as surely as they were seen in the days of our Savior. It seems that the devil has learned that he can sink more souls into perdition by leading them to wallow in depression, cling to their addictions, and to commit suicide, among many other things, than to possess them by taking full control of their bodies. Demons still possess people today, though it seems more subtle. The serpent has only grown in his ability to deceive.

But we have a defense against these attacks. It is outlined in the sixth chapter of Ephesians. We need spiritual armor and a special weapon to "withstand in the evil day" (Ephesians 6:13). To stand protected, we need truth, righteousness, a missionary spirit, faith, a personal relationship with God, dependence on Scripture, and an attitude of prayer.

Demonic forces still oppose me even as I seek to expose their workings. At the same camp meeting that I attended with Jenni, while I was absorbed in getting to know her and preparing my testimony, I was not aware of the evil that was so near. I discovered it the following spring during a wilderness retreat where I was a speaker. A teenager, Anna, came up to me and wanted to talk. She was at the family camp meeting the previous October and had heard me speak. She was born into a family that practiced witchcraft and spoke with demons on a daily basis. At age six, though she lived with Christian parents, she began to speak to these demons so that they would stop tormenting her. They gave her unnaturally good feelings and protected her from her sister's abuse. Anna related that when she was ten years old, the demons weren't acting so friendly and she wanted to stop communicating with them, but they would not let her. Now at sixteen she wrote:

I was 14 when something happened that changed my life. I became rebellious against my parents and God. I felt He wasn't helping me out of this situation with the dark world and the abuse. I had been playing violin since I was six. It has always been a gift, because I play by ear and it just comes to me. I knew it was a gift from God and yet I wanted to play ungodly music. You see, I had made a commitment to God that if He helped me play by ear, I would only play for His honor and glory. But unfortunately, I started listening to ungodly music, which made me want to play this type of music.

One Sabbath afternoon, my parents shared the video Sonic Warfare *by Ivor Myers with some of the youth at the church and they pretty much made me sit through it, which I thank God for now. But at the end of the testimony, Ivor Myers made an altar call. He said that all the musicians watching this video needed to recommit themselves to God. And that really touched my heart.*

That night, as I was going to sleep, I began to feel that strange but yet familiar presence in my room. Satan came to me that night, and showed me famous violin players of the world that played for him, and told me if I was to commit myself to play for him, he would make me famous also. I said, "Get thee behind me, Satan. I serve only one God and that is the true God!" Then he left me alone for about two years.

Anna told me that two years later she began to experience deep depression and eating disorders. Withdrawing from others, she began to see the demons again, although she did not entertain them. She seemed stuck and Satan was telling her that she was not a good person; because of that Jesus wouldn't help her.

Then she shared about her experience at the October camp meeting. Her family usually helps with camp meetings and she likes hanging out with her friends that she only sees once a year. One of her friends who knew me told her about my presentation that evening.

He told me that you had dealt with spiritualism as well and thought that listening to you might help me.

I made up an excuse of being too tired to go to the meeting that night. But he didn't give up. He kept asking me over and over to please go to the meeting that night, so I did. I really wasn't tired at all.

I finally agreed to go, but as I was sitting through the meeting I began to feel so sleepy that I couldn't keep my eyes open. Suddenly I began to feel the presence that I recognized so well. Then there, near the piano, was the dark, shadowy figure. And I felt embarrassed because I had allowed that presence to be there by my own actions. My friend noticed that there was something wrong with me and asked me what was going on. I told him that nothing was wrong. He then asked if I minded if we prayed. And after prayer the presence immediately left. I then realized that God really wanted me to listen to your testimony. I got a great blessing out of it. It truly changed my life.

I was able to share some specific things that God has shown me about fighting the forces of evil and how not to give place to the devil's attacks. I showed her the scriptures that spoke of our spiritual warfare and that God was looking for young people like her to take a stand for Him and be a witness for His power. As one of my favorite quotes states:

The greatest want of the world is the want of men—men who will not be bought or sold, men who in their inmost souls are true and honest, men who do not fear to call sin by its right name, men whose conscience is as true to duty as the needle to the pole, men who will stand for the right though the heavens fall. (*Education*, 57)

Chapter 35
BE THOU MY VISION

After my proposal to Jenni, we began seeing providences everywhere we turned; God was leading. As we contemplated our future, we saw God open doors left and right. First, we found the perfect place to rent for her until we got married, and her house in Georgia was rented out before she moved in March. Then, she found a good paying nanny job before she even arrived.

We shared so many things in common. From the beginning, God had been preparing us for each other. Besides our brown curly hair, we figured out that we were baptized just eleven days apart, me on November 27 and Jenni on December 8, 2001. Jenni had spent many summers working as a colporteur, or literature evangelist. She loved ministry and I loved ministry too. Together we determined to be a team in witnessing for our Savior.

On June 16, 2013, while the Nebbletts, a godly young family, played the tune of *Be Thou My Vision*, John Lane, Jenni's father, walked her down the aisle toward me. Had this day really come? Could it be that God favored me so much? Solomon wrote, and he would know, "He who finds a wife finds a good thing, and obtains favor from the LORD" (Proverbs 18:22). I was favored that day! Hand in hand we exchanged our vows and committed to each other for life. We walked out of the same church that I first walked into the Sabbath after my release from prison.

Since that time, the miracles have continued unabated. God continues to show Himself strong in the Allen family.

During my two-year tenure as a Bible worker, I was able to witness many of my students yield fully to God and be baptized into His remnant church. I was called to be a local elder and became a regular Sabbath school teacher.

I had long desired to receive further training in how to labor for souls, but saw no clear way open to receive it. That was until friend after friend encouraged me to attend the Amazing Facts Center of

Evangelism (AFCOE). Financially it was impossible because of my growing family. It was also unlikely simply because of my criminal background. But God isn't hindered by these things. I received a letter of acceptance into the fall 2014 class, a class that assisted with the Landmarks of Prophecy series presented by Doug Batchelor in Albuquerque, New Mexico.

All of those encouraging friends who supported our ministry with their mouths then supported us with their wallets. Sponsorship money poured in, not to mention Debbie Sue, our 2008 Toyota Sienna that was donated to us by Debbie and her mom, Sue. They said, "May it be a tank for the Lord."

The miracle money was raised, and the miracle van was packed. We were on our way to an incredible soul-winning and evangelism training school. Sure, it was like drinking water from a fire hydrant, but I was a thirsty soul! Our classes were taught by the finest teachers in Adventism. Chuck Holtry, the director of AFCOE, was a personal mentor and now is a good friend. What more could I ask for?

But then the next miracle happened. Amazing Facts was looking for another evangelist to go on the road preaching the three angels' messages. Unworthy though I felt, I recognized the voice of God, and as a family we accepted the call. Our first mission: Nepal! Carissa McSherry led the AFCOE team, and her sister Desiree lead the AMEN (Adventist Medical Evangelism Network) team. AMEN ministers to physical needs, and AFCOE ministers to spiritual needs. Our work in Nepal repeatedly demonstrated to me how the medical missionary work should always be connected with the evangelistic work.

The evangelistic work is great, but an even greater calling that I have been given is that of being a husband and father. God has blessed Jenni and me with a beautiful baby daughter, Purity Patience Allen. Like those in the Bible whose names signify their character, we aim to develop in her the fruits of the Spirit, even as they are developed in us. May we be found faithful with our new charge, may the angels always delight to be in our home, and may God's favor continue to rest on our family and ministry.

Chapter 36
GOING FORWARD

B eing a criminal was not something I wanted to be when I grew up. As bad as I was, none of my school yearbooks said "Wyatt Allen—Most likely to end up in prison." Nor can I say that it was my folks or my background that caused me to wind up behind bars. I chose a life of rebellion and reaped the whirlwind because of it. I deserved worse than I received. Let none think that the Lord's hand is shortened, that it cannot save (See Isaiah 59:1). I live to tell the wonderful story of Jesus and His love.

"And they overcame him by the blood of the Lamb and by the word of their testimony, and they did not love their lives to the death'" (Revelation 12:11). Looking back on what God has done in my life gives me the confidence that He is going to do even greater things in the future. My "rap-sheet," or criminal record, in heaven has been washed clean by the blood of Jesus, even if my earthly one is still stained.

Mine is a testimony of God's saving power. Yes, He saved me from a corrupt and degenerate past, but there is a testimony that is much greater than mine, one that I love to hear. This is the testimony of God's keeping power. I would rather tell the story of being raised by godly parents, staying in the church, and always being faithful to God. In fact, I want to make both testimonies mine. God is calling for people everywhere to avail themselves of His divine power to save and to keep. "Now unto Him that is able to keep you from falling, and to present you faultless before the presence of His glory with exceeding joy, to the only wise God our Saviour, be glory and majesty, dominion and power, both now and ever. Amen" (Jude 24, 25 KJV).

My future is still being written, as is yours. Each day is another opportunity to serve the God of love. He has led me to the doors of many souls hungering and thirsting for righteousness. I have seen several souls buried in the waters of baptism as the fruit of my work for Him, and I hope to see more soon as I prepare to preach my first evangelistic series. I wonder how He can use such a broken vessel, but I pause to remember that with God nothing is impossible. I feel honored to be in His service and count it great joy to be used by Him.

God is at work today and is calling all who will, to minister for Him in His vineyard. The three angels' messages must go all around the world, to every nation, kindred, tongue, and people. "And this gospel of the kingdom will be preached in all the world as a witness to all the nations, and then the end will come" (Matthew 24:14). Jesus is coming back to set us free from this old world! Then will Satan and his hosts, whom I used to serve, will be bound for a thousand-year prison sentence. This time will not change them, but will confirm them in their rebellion. Then the devil and all his followers will receive the death sentence "and shall be no more forever" (Ezekiel 28:19).

"The LORD hath appeared of old unto me, saying, Yea, I have loved thee with an everlasting love: therefore with lovingkindness have I drawn thee." God's love won me to the truth. And now "the love of Christ compels" me to share this love with others (Jeremiah 31:3 KJV; 2 Corinthians 5:14). I rejoice that I serve a living Savior who was not ashamed to accept me, even me, the least of the least.

APPENDICES

Appendix 1: What happens after death?

- We are made from the dust and God's breath/spirit: Genesis 2:7.

- When we die the reverse happens: Ecclesiastes 12:7 (notice this is for everyone, not just believers).

- The body without the spirit (breath) is dead: James 2:26.

- Breath and spirit mean the same thing in this context: Job 27:3.

- The soul is a combination of breath and dust: Genesis 2:7.

- Souls can die: Ezekiel 18:20; Revelation 16:3.

- Man is mortal (subject to death): Job 4:17; 1 Timothy 6:15, 16.

- People are in their graves until Jesus comes: John 5:28, 29.

- David is not in heaven now: Acts 2:29, 34.

- The grave is the holding place until the end: Job 17:13.

- The dead are unconscious and know nothing: Ecclesiastes 9:5, 6, 10.

- The dead do not praise the Lord: Psalm 115:17.

- The dead are not conscious of things on earth: Job 14:12, 21.

- Their thoughts have perished: Psalm 146:4.

- Jesus calls death a sleep: John 11:11–14.

- As it is elsewhere called sleep: 1 Kings 11:21 (KJV); Psalm 13:3; 1 Corinthians 11:30; 15:51; Ephesians 5:14.

- The dead do not awaken until "the heavens are no more" (Job 14:12), which is when the Lord will come: 2 Peter 3:10.

- The righteous dead are not raised until the second corning: Revelation 22:12; 1 Thessalonians 4:16, 17; 1 Corinthians 15:51–53.

- Satan's lie teaches that the dead are conscience or alive: Genesis 3:4; Revelation 12:9.

- Satan deceives through a false understanding of death: Exodus 7:11; 1 Samuel 28:3–25; Daniel 2:2; Matthew 24:23, 24; Acts 16:16–18; 2 Corinthians 11:13, 14; Revelation 13:13, 14; 16:14; 18:23. Correctly understanding God's Word is our protection: Acts 17:11; Isaiah 8:20.

- God commanded the death penalty for those who believed and taught that the dead were alive: Leviticus 20:27.

Appendix 2: How long will hell burn?

- Hell is not burning now: 2 Peter 2:9.

- Hell will be at the end of this age: Matthew 13:40–42; John 12:48; John 5:28, 29; Job 21:30–32; Revelation 20:9.

- Only the righteous receive immortality, not the wicked (would God give the wicked eternal life just to keep them suffering?): Romans 6:23; James 1:15; John 3:16; Genesis 3:22–24; 1 Timothy 6:14–16; 1 Corinthians 15:51–54; Job 4:17.

- Hell, or the lake of fire, is called the "second death" (not life): Revelation 21:8.

- The Bible describes the destruction of the wicked in no uncertain terms:

- The wicked suffer death: Romans 6:23.

- The wicked suffer destruction: Job 21:30.

- The wicked will perish: Psalm 37:20.

- The wicked will burn up: Malachi 4:1.

- The wicked will be destroyed together: Psalm 37:38.

- The wicked vanish away: Psalm 37:20.

- The wicked will be cut off: Psalm 37:9.

- The wicked will be slain: Psalm 62:3.

- God will destroy the wicked: Psalm 62:3.

- Fire will devour them: Psalm 21:9.

- They will be as though they had never been: Obadiah 1:16.

- God will leave them neither root nor branch: Malachi 4:1.

- Hell will burn on this earth (which the saints will later inherit): Proverbs 11:31; Revelation 20:9; Matthew 13:40–42; 2 Peter 3:10.

- The wicked will only receive what they deserve as individuals: Revelation 22:12; Matthew 16:27; Luke 12:47, 48.

- The fire will eventually go out: Isaiah 47:14; Revelation 21:1, 4.

- The wicked will not continue to live but will be turned into ashes after the fire has gone out: Malachi 4:1, 3; Psalm 37:10, 20.

- Hell will literally burn the wicked in a physical way: Matthew 5:30; Matthew 10:28; Ezekiel 18:20.

- Even the devil will eventually cease to exist after being burned up: Revelation 20:10; Ezekiel 28:18, 19.

- Hell's purpose is to destroy the devil and his angels and the sinners who follow them, not to perpetuate them throughout all eternity: Matthew 25:41; Revelation 20:15; Psalm 37:10, 20.

- God loves the wicked and doesn't want to destroy them (though He will if they fail to repent): Ezekiel 33:11; Luke 9:56; Isaiah 28:21.

- Forever doesn't always mean without end: Jonah 2:6; Matthew 12:39; Revelation 11:15; 1 Corinthians 15:25; Exodus 28:43; Hebrews 7:11; Deuteronomy 23:3–5; Nehemiah 13:1; Ecclesiastes 1:4; Matthew 5:18; 1 Samuel 1:22, 28; 1 Samuel 25:1; Deuteronomy 15:17.

Appendix 3: The Lord set apart the seventh day of the week as the Sabbath and has never repealed it.

- God made the Sabbath after creation week: Genesis 1:1; 2:2, 3.

- God wrote the Sabbath commandment on stone with His own finger with the rest of the Ten Commandments: Exodus 20:8–11; Deuteronomy 9:10.

- The Ten Commandments have never been changed: Luke 16:17; Psalm 89:34; Exodus 20:1. (God spoke the Ten Commandments from His own lips.)

- Jesus kept the seventh-day Sabbath: Luke 4:16.

- The Apostles kept the Sabbath: Acts 17:2; Acts 13:13, 14; Acts 16:13; Acts 18:4.

- Even the Gentiles were to keep the day holy: Isaiah 56:2, 6, 7; Acts 13:42, 44; Acts 18:4.

- God blessed the Sabbath: Exodus 20:11; Genesis 2:3.

- Jesus expected His people to still be keeping the day holy in A.D. 70 when Jerusalem was destroyed: Matthew 24:20.

- The women kept the Sabbath even after Jesus' death: Mark 15:37, 42; Luke 23:56; Mark 16:2.

- Luke called the seventh-day the Sabbath, not the first day of the week (Sunday)—and he was a Gentile: Luke 23:54–56.

- The Sabbath was made for all mankind, not just the Jews: Mark 2:27; Genesis 2:2–4.

- The Sabbath will be kept in the new heavens and new earth: Isaiah 66:22, 23.

- The only day called the Lord's Day in the Bible is the seventh-day Sabbath, not Sunday or the first day of the week: Revelation 1:10; Isaiah 58:13; Matthew 12:8; Mark 2:28; Exodus 20:10.

- Christians honor the resurrection of Jesus through baptism, not by trying to make a day holy that God never commanded: Romans 6:3–6.

- We honor Christ by obeying Him: John 14:15.

- Long-standing traditions should never replace God's commandments: Mark 7:9–13; Matthew 15:3–9; Colossians 2:8.

- Sunday-keeping is a tradition of those who would tamper with the Word of God as foretold in Daniel 7:25; Matthew 15:6, 9; and Ezekiel 22:26, 28.

- No man can reverse God's blessing on the Sabbath: Numbers 23:20; 1 Chronicles 17:27.

- We are not to add to God's Word or law: Deuteronomy 4:2; Proverbs 30:5, 6.

- The Sabbath was made to be a sign between God and His people: Exodus 20:8, 11; Ezekiel 20:12, 20; Exodus 31:13, 17; Isaiah 58:13, 14.

- Sabbath-breaking is law-breaking: 1 John 3:4; James 2:10; 1 Peter 2:21; Hebrews 5:9.

- God does not look too fondly on the religious leaders who ignore the Sabbath: Ezekiel 22:26–31; Mark 7:7–13; James 3:1; Matthew 15:14.

- What should our attitude be about the Sabbath? John 14:15; 1 John 5:3.

- The last-day church will be a commandment-keeping church, which includes the Sabbath: Revelation 12:17; 14:12; 22:14.

Appendix 4: God is truly concerned about our health. He wants the best for us.

- God wants above all things for us to be healthy: 3 John 2.

- He gave us health rules for "our good always, that He might preserve us alive": Deuteronomy 6:24; Exodus 23:25; John 10:10.

- God expressly commands us: "Eat what is good": Isaiah 55:2.

- Do all to the glory of God: 1 Corinthians 10:31.

- He holds nothing good back from His people: Psalm 84:11.

- God's original diet was fruit, grains, and nuts. Vegetables were added later: Genesis 1:29; 2:16; 3:18.

- After God allowed meat eating He had specifically forbidden certain animals:

   (1) All animals which do not have a split hoof and chew the cud: Deuteronomy 14:6.

(2) All fish and water creatures that do not have both fins and scales: Deuteronomy 14:9.

(3) All birds of prey, carrion eaters, and fish eaters: Leviticus 11:13-20.

(4) Most "creeping things" (or invertebrates) are also unclean: Leviticus 11:21-47. Some of the popular unclean (filthy, unhealthy) animals are rabbits, squirrels, catfish, pigs, lobsters, clams, crabs, shrimp, oysters, frogs, etc. God expressly forbids swine (pigs): Isaiah 66:15, 16; 65:2–5.

- These rules date back to before the Jews and Moses' time: Genesis 7:1, 2.

- We are not to touch what is unclean: 2 Corinthians 6:17.

- Unclean people are not accepted with God: Ephesians 5:5.

- John likens Babylon to a holding place for unclean animals: Revelation 18:2.

- God has a reward for those who continue to desire detestable things and their abominations: Ezekiel 11:21.

- God never blesses what he calls an abomination (think about homosexuality: Leviticus 18:22, or idolatry: Deuteronomy 7:25): Leviticus 11; Deuteronomy 14.

- We are to cleanse ourselves from all filthiness of the flesh and spirit: 2 Corinthians 7:1.

- There will be no meat eating in the new heavens and new earth: Isaiah 65:21, 25; 11:9.

Appendix 5: The gift of tongues was given to the church to build it up, but it has been twisted and counterfeited. What does the Bible say about this wonderful gift?

- This gift, like the others, was to be for the equipping of the saints for ministry: Ephesians 4:8–16.

- Tongues were to be for a sign for unbelievers: 1 Corinthians 14:22.

- The true evidence of being born again for believers is the fruit of righteousness: Matthew 7:16–20; Galatians 5:22, 23; Ephesians 5:9; 1 John 2:2–5; John 13:35.

- When the Holy Spirit was poured out, it was in actual languages understood by foreigners: Acts 2:2–16.

- God gave the gift of tongues to Cornelius' house and to the Ephesians twelve: Acts 10; Acts 19; Acts 11:15–18; Acts 15:7–9.

- People did not always speak with tongues in the book of Acts when they received the Holy Spirit: Acts 4:31; Acts 18:16, 17; Acts 9:17, 18.

- Tongues were one of the many gifts given to the church: 1 Corinthians 12:28–30.

- Not everyone received this gift: 1 Corinthians 12:30.

- The Holy Spirit decides who receives what gift: 1 Corinthians 12:7, 8, 18, 28. 1 Corinthians 14:1–5 says prophecy is to be preferred over the gift of tongues. Tongue speaking wasn't doing anyone any good if no one could understand what was being said. Thus we see Paul's rebuke in verses 2 and 4. In verses 6–19, Paul says that tongues are useless unless somebody is being edified. Paul's burden was that "it be known what is spoken" (verse 9). This chapter is talking about real human languages (verse 10). Verses 20–25 again clarify the purpose of this gift: a sign to unbelievers. Paul wanted the Corinthians to conduct church in an orderly fashion, but speaking in an unfamiliar language causes confusion: 1 Corinthians 14:26–40.

- We are to avoid babbling: Matthew 6:7, 8; 1 Timothy 1:6; 6:20; 2 Timothy 2:16; Genesis 11.

- We are to abstain from all appearance of evil: 1 Thessalonians 5:22.

Appendix 6: My study on races and racism resulted in these following findings:

- We are all descended from one man and are of one race: Acts 17:26.

- And all these descendants were made in the image of God: Genesis 1:26, 27; 9:6; 1 Corinthians 11:7.

- Man looks at the outward appearance, but the LORD looks at the heart: 1 Samuel 16:7.

- God specifically condemns the spirit of bigotry, elitism, racism, partiality, and discrimination: James 1:1–13.

- Christians are one in Christ: Galatians 3:28, 29; Ephesians 2:14:22; Romans 10:12; Colossians 3:11.

- We are to love our neighbor as ourselves: Matthew 22:39; Luke 6:31; Matthew 7:12.

- Our neighbor is anyone we come in contact with, specifically those of other nationalities: Luke 10:27–27.

- All humanity was destroyed in the global flood except eight people who were told to repopulate the earth and from whom we are all descended: Genesis 6:7, 13; 7:4, 23; 9:1.

- The Great Commission (Matthew 28:19) and the Day of Pentecost (Acts 2:5–11) illustrate God's plan to reach across language and cultural barriers: Acts 8:26–39.

- The three angels' messages go to every nation, tribe, tongue, and people: Revelation 14:6.

- The command to not intermarry with other nations refers not to the race but to the faith; God has allowed those to come in who adopt the faith of Israel: Deuteronomy 7:3, 4; Judges 3:6; 1 Kings 11:1–8; Ezra 9:10–12; Exodus 22:21; Leviticus 19:32–34; Exodus 12:48, 49; Numbers 9:14; 15:14; Ruth 1:16; 4:13, 17.

- The promise to Abraham was to bless all the nations of the earth: Genesis 22:18.

- Jesus wanted His Father's house to be a house of prayer for all nations: Mark 11:17; Isaiah 56:7.

- The promise of salvation is for the whole world, not just a select few: John 3:16; 12:32.

- God shows no partiality: Acts 10:34, 35.

- Heaven will have people of all nations, tribes, peoples, and tongues: Revelation 7:9.

- We are commanded to seek justice and confront oppression everywhere: Deuteronomy 16:19; Isaiah 1:17; Jeremiah 22:3.

- If we hate, we are in darkness: 1 John 2:9–11.

Albert Allen (Dad), 1974,
official Marine Corp photo

Albert Allen (Dad)
and Grandma
Ella Mae

Wyatt at 6 months

Wyatt (14), 1997

Dustin (4) and
Wyatt (2), 1985

*Jefferson City News
Tribune* clipping
about arson fire,
see page 17

Four juveniles in custody for setting fires

Four juveniles were taken into custody Thursday in connection with a fire that occurred Aug. 8 at 715 E. Miller St.

Police said the four range in age from 6 to 11.

A police spokesman said the four were building fires in the area, and one of the fires got away from them. The children were setting fires in a cemetery, which led to them coming to police attention, the spokesman said, adding that the children had been seen in the area of the East Miller Street fire.

The structure at 715 E. Miller was destroyed by the blaze. It was unoccupied at the time of the fire, police said.

The four juveniles have been questioned and are awaiting a juvenile court hearing.

Jasmine (9), Dustin (14),
Joe (15), Wyatt (12),
Nicole (11 months), 1995

Dustin (5) and
Wyatt (3), 1986

Dustin (16), Jasmine (10), Wyatt
(14), Nicole (2), 1996

Mom, Wyatt (9),
Jasmine (6),
Dustin (11), 1992

Giving Mom away to stepdad Mike,
Dustin (12), Wyatt (10), 1993

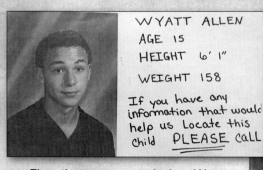

WYATT ALLEN
AGE 15
HEIGHT 6' 1"
WEIGHT 158

If you have any information that would help us Locate this child PLEASE CALL

Flyer that mom posted when Wyatt
went missing, see page 21

Wyatt (16), jail booking
photo, June 24, 1999,
see page 31

Mom, Wyatt (19), 2002

Wyatt (20), Amy (20), 2003

Actual *Great Controversy* and *Strong's Concordance* used by Wyatt in prison, see pages 47, 55, 74

Wyatt's Sign Language Class, 2003, see pages 115, 134

Church friends: Sharon,
Wyatt (24), David Misenko, 2007

Visiting the least of the least:
Pastor Dan, Jean Paxon,
Wyatt (19), Inez Brisendine,
2002, see page 115

Wyatt in prison, re-established
as office clerk after 41 days in
the hole (23), see page 121

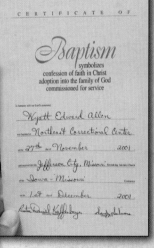

Wyatt's baptismal
certificate, November 27,
2001, see page 115

Prison church group with volunteer John
Stone, Wyatt (20), 2003, see pages 116, 117

Wyatt and Jenni at Camp
Heritage in Lake of the
Ozarks, MO … first time meeting in
person, 2012, see pages 155–157

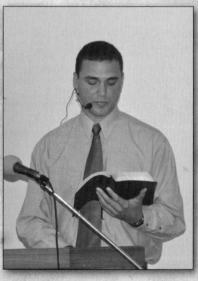

Wyatt preaching at family camp,
2012, see pages 155–157

Wyatt at camp meeting,
2012, see pages 155–157

Jenni, night of marriage proposal… she said "Yes!" January 1, 2013, see page 160

All grown up: Dustin, Wyatt, Joe, Jasmine, Nicole, June 16, 2013

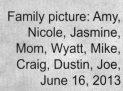

Family picture: Amy, Nicole, Jasmine, Mom, Wyatt, Mike, Craig, Dustin, Joe, June 16, 2013

Without seeing each other before the wedding, Wyatt and Jenni asking God to bless their marriage, June 16, 2013

Wyatt and Jenni wedding, June 16, 2013

Wedding party: Tara, Nicole, Jasmine, Rhina, Lani, Amy, Crystal, Jenni, Wyatt, Doug, Craig, David, Christian, Dustin, Joe, June 16, 2013

Wyatt and Jenni, honeymoon in Costa Rica, 2013

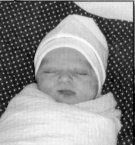

Wyatt and Jenni, June 16, 2013

Purity Patience Allen, one day old, born April 30, 2014

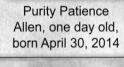

Sabbath afternoon family hike with Purity, three days old, May 3, 2014

The Allen Family

Purity's first teeth